LINCOLN'S SPYMASTER

LINCOLN'S SPYMASTER

Thomas Haines Dudley
and
the Liverpool Network

David Hepburn Milton

STACKPOLE
BOOKS

Published by
STACKPOLE BOOKS
5067 Ritter Road
Mechanicsburg, PA 17055
www.stackpolebooks.com

Printed in the United States of America

10 9 8 7 6 5 4 3 2 1

FIRST EDITION

Library of Congress Cataloging-in-Publication Data

Milton, David Hepburn.
    Lincoln's spymaster : Thomas Haines Dudley and the Liverpool network / David Hepburn Milton.— 1st ed.
      p. cm.
    Includes bibliographical references and index.
    ISBN 0-8117-0015-1
    1. Dudley, Thomas H. (Thomas Haines), 1819–1893. 2. United States—History—Civil War, 1861–1865—Secret service. 3. Spies—United States—Biography. 4. Spies—England—Liverpool—Biography. 5. Espionage, American—England—Liverpool—History—19th century. 6. United States—History—Civil War, 1861–1865—Naval operations. 7. Confederate States of America. Navy—History. 8. United States—Foreign relations—Great Britain. 9. Great Britain—Foreign relations—United States. I. Title.
    E608 .M45 2002
    973.7'57—dc21

                        2002008138

For Nancy
and our forty-year adventure together

CONTENTS

LIST OF ILLUSTRATIONS

Photo Section appears between pages 70 and 71.

ACKNOWLEDGMENTS

My interest in the career of Thomas Haines Dudley was stimulated by reading James M. McPherson's excellent one-volume history of the American Civil War, *Battle Cry of Freedom: The Civil War Era.* I was particularly intrigued by McPherson's description of the U.S. consul at Liverpool as a "combative Quaker" who was engaged in a secret duel with the able head of the Confederate Secret Service, James Dunwoody Bulloch. McPherson described this struggle as "a contest of lawyers, spies and double agents that would furnish material for an espionage thriller."

After some preliminary research, I discovered that there were no biographies of Thomas Dudley and that his story had to be pieced together from monographs and histories of the period. My primary research was done at the Huntington Library in San Marino, California, which holds a wonderful collection of the papers of Thomas Haines Dudley, including all of his Liverpool dispatches. Basing my research on this primary material, I was then able to flesh out the story with the aid of major historians of the diplomatic and international aspects of the Civil War period. I describe these sources in some detail in a bibliographical note at the back of this volume.

I owe a great deal to Tom Engelhardt, my former editor and old, dear friend, who was the first professional to read the whole manuscript and enthusiastically encouraged me to seek its publication. Engelhardt made a number of useful suggestions that I have incorporated in the book. Another friend, John Plotz, a lawyer with literary talent, also made helpful recommendations that I have adopted.

I especially wish to thank William Cameron Davis, a Civil War scholar associated with the Center for Civil War Studies at Virginia Tech, who read the manuscript and recommended it for publication by Stackpole Books. Leigh Ann Berry, editor at Stackpole Books, patiently and expertly expedited the complex process of publication from start to finish. It was a pleasure to work with her, and I also thank editorial assistant Ryan Masteller and copyeditor Joyce Bond, for their professional help in improving the manuscript

I am indebted to John Rhodehamel, Norris Foundation Curator of American History at the Huntington Library, who photocopied all the illustrations scattered among the Dudley papers and forwarded them to me. A number of these illustrations of Confederate ships are included in this book, and I thank the Huntington Library for permission for their reproduction. I wish to thank Eric Daird, Trainer for Computing Services at Southern Oregon University, for his patient and expert advice that allowed me to conquer some complex computer problems with the manuscript.

Finally, I am fortunate to be married to a writer and English teacher whose professional expertise has been indispensable to my writing over many decades.

INTRODUCTION

HISTORIANS OF THE AMERICAN CIVIL WAR DISAGREE AS TO WHETHER THAT war was essentially a domestic conflict or an international event. However, the dean of Civil War historians, Allan Nevins, had no doubts on this question, writing: "No battle, not Gettysburg, not the Wilderness, was more important than the contest waged in the diplomatic arena and the forum of public opinion."[1]

This book attempts to illuminate a crucial overseas theater of the diplomatic and intelligence war between the North and South during the American Civil War. The focus is on the dual strategic effort of the South to win Britain as an ally while at the same time constructing a state-of-the-art Confederate naval fleet in British shipyards, a strategy that was brilliantly countered by Thomas Haines Dudley, Lincoln's consul at Liverpool. Without Dudley, the North might well have lost the struggle to prevent the construction of a Confederate navy in British shipyards. The Quaker lawyer from New Jersey may well be seen as the father of modern American intelligence operations on the international front that combine covert with conventional diplomatic strategies.

The birth of the United States emerged from a centuries-long international conflict among European imperial powers, primarily the English, French, Dutch, Spanish, and Portuguese. Thus, as this book argues, the American Civil War could be considered the last act in the epic struggle among European nations for dominance in North America. It was this second American Revolution, a war involving the most modern technology of its day, from which the United States arose as a major world power.

For more than two hundred years, European powers fought for control of the North American continent. In the seventeenth century, English expansion in New England clashed with French imperial designs in the North, Spanish claims in the South, and Dutch control of the Hudson River Valley. New France, New England, New Netherlands, and New Spain were all products of the mercantilist system that led to war among the great powers of the time. From the beginning, the evolution of the United States as a modern nation was a product of international forces.

In his seminal research on the origins of North American settlement, Bernard Bailyn argues that "in the end the massive transfer to the Western Hemisphere of people from Africa, from the European mainland, and above all from the Anglo-Celtic offshore islands of Europe" culminated "in what Bismark called 'the decisive fact of the modern world.'"[2]

Historians Richard Hofstadter, William Miller, and David Aaron agree that "virtually from the beginning of settlement in North America, the Protestant British and the Catholic Spanish and French, each with their tentative Indian allies, had been warring with one another. The central issue in the enduring conflict was nothing less than the role and purpose of the New World in the European scheme of things."[3]

North America was, therefore, only one front in a world war being fought among shifting European alliances. In the mid-seventeenth century, Britain, Portugal, and Prussia were aligned against France, Austria, Sweden, Russia, and Spain. This world conflict was fought out in Europe and the Mediterranean, the West Indies, the Indian Ocean and the far Pacific, as well as throughout North America. The American Revolution and the establishment of the United States of America can only be understood as a direct outcome of the continuing global war among the great nations of Europe.[4]

After early defeats by the French and their Indian allies in what is commonly called the French and Indian War, the British finally won a decisive victory over the French at Quebec. In 1763, Britain and France signed the Treaty of Paris, in which the French ceded all of Canada and the interior of North America east of the Mississippi. France obtained the islands of Guadeloupe and Martinique in the West Indies, and Spain gave up Florida to the British in exchange for Cuba. Britain, with the use of its main forces and Colonial troops, including George Washington, had won major control of the North American heartland. Nevertheless, the global struggle between Britain and France continued for another century.

France achieved its revenge on Britain by forging an alliance with the American Revolutionary army under Washington. Without French troops and the French Navy, General Washington would never have been able to win his final victory against the British at Yorktown. It is clear that the American colonists in their fight for independence succeeded mainly because they were able to create a strategy based on the conflict among the great European powers. Thomas Jefferson appeared to have achieved American domination of the North American continent by his purchase of the Louisiana Territory from France in 1803. However, during the American Civil War, the Confederate States hoped to achieve independence by winning intervention from the British and French as allies.

Parallel to the imperial struggle for control of North America was the complex conflict among the three races inhabiting the territory of the United States. In his classic study, *Democracy in America,* Tocqueville described the conditions of white supremacy shaping the new nation. Characterizing the American Indians and African-Americans as "two unhappy races," Tocqueville declares that both "occupy an equally inferior position in the country they inhabit; both suffer from tyranny; and if their wrongs are not the same, they originate from the same authors." He concludes: "If we reason from what passes in the world, we should say that the European is to the other races of mankind what man himself is to the lower animals: he makes them subservient to his use, and when he cannot subdue he destroys them."[5]

Democracy and racism, two contradictory components of American life, have been tragically linked throughout the whole course of American history. Nevertheless, at particular historical turning points, European whites forged alliances with American Indians and African blacks against a common enemy. Indian tribes made alliances with both the French and the British against expanding European settlements and Colonial rebellion. In the long run, however, Native Americans became the victims of genocidal wars of extermination carried out by European white settlers determined to dominate the North American continent.

African-Americans who had endured almost two hundred years of slavery by white Europeans were able to achieve a historical alliance with the Northern white nation to defeat the Confederate slave system during the American Civil War. Lincoln's Emancipation Proclamation was, in fact, a military strategy required for victory in the war against the South. As James McPherson describes it: "Lincoln had embraced emancipation both as a way to weaken the Confederacy by depriving it of slave labor and as a sweeping expansion of Union war aims. No longer would the North fight merely for restoration of the old Union—a union where slavery flouted American ideals of liberty. Now the North would fight to give that Union 'a new birth of liberty,' as Lincoln put it almost a year later at Gettysburg."[6] McPherson further argues that the "organization of black regiments marked the transformation of a war to preserve the Union into a revolution to overthrow the old order."[7]

While racial struggle and alliance determined the politics of the American Civil War, the war as an international event provided the European powers one last chance to shape historical outcomes in North America. Prominent leaders in Britain, in particular Foreign Minister Lord John Russell and Chancellor of the Exchequer William Gladstone, believed that Southern independence was inevitable and were ready to intervene to guarantee such an outcome. "British intervention," as the historian Howard Jones points out, "would probably have led to an Anglo-American war."[8] The potential of British intervention on the side of the South and the parallel threat of an advanced Confederate navy constructed in British shipyards made Liverpool and London strategic fronts of Northern diplomacy and espionage.

Spain, in turn, took advantage of the American conflict to reannex Santo Domingo. When a British diplomat warned that the United States might resist this new Spanish intervention in the Caribbean, a Spanish official replied, "The United States of today are very different from that they were a year ago; they have differences of their own to settle."[9] France also took advantage of the American Civil War to invade Mexico, capture Mexico City, and install a puppet government under the Austrian archduke Ferdinand Maximilian.

A major hope of the South and fear of the North was British and French official recognition of the sovereignty of the Confederacy followed by European military intervention to guarantee the establishment of two separate nations out of the former United States. Responsibility for the Union's strategic struggle on the international front during the Civil War lay in the hands of President Lincoln, Secretary of State William H. Seward, the U.S. minister to London, Charles Francis Adams, and the American consul at Liverpool, Thomas Haines Dudley.

Soon after his arrival in England in late November 1861, Dudley emerged as the *de facto* head of Northern intelligence operations in Europe. An obscure lawyer from New Jersey, Dudley had played a key role in the nomination of Abraham Lincoln for president and was rewarded by the new president with the Liverpool appointment. As an ardent abolitionist and activist, diplomat and spymaster, Dudley clearly represented both the international and antislavery character of the American Civil War.

On May 13, 1861, one month after the outbreak of war between the Northern Union and the newly established Southern Confederacy, Britain issued a proclamation of neutrality that granted the status of belligerent to the South. In June, France followed suit with a similar declaration. The French under Napoleon III expressed continued interest in a joint intervention with the British in the American war. In an angry response, Secretary of State Seward warned both countries of the possibility of war with the United States. If other nations intervened, Seward declared, the American conflict would become "a war of the world."[10] Charles Sumner, chairman of the Senate Foreign Relations Committee, called the British action "the most hateful act of English history since the time of Charles 2nd."[11]

Following the Southern attack on Fort Sumter, Confederate president Jefferson Davis announced the licensing of privateers. President Lincoln responded on April 19 with his proclamation of a Northern blockade of all Southern ports by the Union navy and the threat to hang privateers as pirates. The major goal of Washington's foreign policy was to prevent British recognition of the Confederacy. For the South, recognition by Britain and France, followed by European intervention in the conflict on the side of the Confederacy, was a strategic war aim. Richmond was desperate to break the Northern blockade and hoped to utilize Europe's dependence on Southern cotton, and thus by cotton diplomacy win European intervention. Without such foreign intervention, the South could have little hope of victory in the war. Thus, the "Lincoln administration had to block foreign intervention even at the risk of threatening war with England."[12]

From the very beginning of the war, British politicians and leaders of public opinion believed that the United States had been split permanently and that Southern separation was unalterable. The British government, led by Henry John Temple, Lord Palmerston, with its declaration of neutrality, made preparations for dealing with two separate American nations. Most British leaders considered Lincoln a provincial nonentity and Secretary of State Seward a proponent of American expansionism and a dangerous and unscrupulous diplomat.

Britain had outlawed the slave trade in 1833, and moral outrage against the institution of slavery had deep roots in English public opinion. Lincoln's initial declaration that the American Civil War concerned union rather than slavery only reinforced the idea widespread in England that the war was about empire, not slavery. "By bowing to domestic pressure and steering around the slavery issue, Lincoln relieved the British from having to make a decision between their moral commitment to antislavery and their economic interests in Southern cotton."[13]

In fact, Britain's governing classes displayed a decided sympathy for the South. As one historian notes, "The British had reason to look with particular coldness upon the Northern states."[14] The British dislike for the North rested on England's two previous wars with the United States, the Northern call for annexation of Canada during the secession crisis, and the growing industrial competition between England and the Northern Union, reinforced by the Congressional enactment of the Morrill Tariff at the beginning of the war. British distaste for the North was reciprocated by the traditional hostility toward Britain of Northern public opinion.

There is little question that the British aristocracy shared an affinity with the patrician elite of the South and opposed those prominent voices in England that wished to use the American republic as a model for British parliamentary reform. In the first year of the American Civil War, a consensus existed among most classes in Britain that the war would be short and that Southern independence was simply a *fait accompli.* As the war dragged on, Northern military defeats raised British public speculation that foreign intervention was imminent. The *Times* of London, an organ representing the opinion of Prime Minister Palmerston, protested against the continuation of "this horrible war," called upon the British people to throw their "whole moral weight to the South," and demanded that the South be allowed to secede peacefully.[15]

Prime Minister Palmerston and Foreign Secretary Russell, however, inclined to intervene at various times during the first three years of the American Civil War, were held in check by their traditional rivalry with France; by William Seward's determination to resist by force any foreign intervention in the war, followed by a threat to annex Canada; and finally, by a divided cabinet that refused a majority vote for intervention. The threat of intervention persisted throughout the war, however, and continued Confederate military victories no doubt would have guaranteed it. For Charles Francis Adams and Thomas Haines Dudley, commanders of the international front at London and Liverpool, the threat was real and unremitting.

Dudley arrived in Liverpool to take up his post as U.S. consul in late November 1861, just at the height of the *Trent* crisis. While he was still at sea en route to England, an American warship under the command of Charles Wilkes had intercepted the neutral British ship *Trent,* on which two Confederate diplomats, James Mason of Virginia and John Slidell of Louisiana, had taken passage. Captain Wilkes fired two shots across the bow of the *Trent,* stopped the ship, and then sent officers aboard, who removed Mason and Slidell as "the embodiment of dispatches" or contraband. The *Trent* was allowed to resume its course, while Mason, Slidell, and their two secretaries were taken to Boston and locked up in Fort Warren.

Wilkes's action was unprecedented and a clear violation of international law.[16] Outraged British public opinion overwhelmingly supported the Palmerston government's demand for a formal apology from Washington and the immediate release of the prisoners. Responding to the crisis, Britain prepared for war with the Union by sending thousands of troops to Canada and enlarging its Atlantic fleet. The *Trent* affair was finally resolved by the decision of the Lincoln cabinet to release the two diplomats, followed by a public declaration that Wilkes's action had been unauthorized and by an able dispatch by Secretary of State Seward that succeeded in breaking the British-American impasse while retaining American honor.

Upon taking up his post in Liverpool, Thomas Dudley found himself in the middle of a war crisis in Britain's major port city, which had become a Confederate stronghold. Confederate agents had already succeeded in initiating the construction of Southern warships in English shipyards. After a few months in office, Dudley would write Secretary of State Seward that "the people of this place if not the entire Kingdom seem to be becoming every day more and more enlisted" in the service of the Confederacy.[17]

Dudley immediately set to work to establish an intelligence network capable of uncovering detailed information concerning all warships under construction in Great Britain for the South and identifying blockade runners chartered to the Confederacy. In a short period of time, the Liverpool consul had a team of spies made up of British shipyard workers and other sympathizers to the Northern cause, British private detectives, and paid informers, who uncovered every aspect of Confederate secret activities in Britain. Soon there was neither a Confederate ship under construction nor a blockade runner that escaped Dudley's scrutiny. Dudley's timely and consistent dispatches to the State and Navy Departments on the date and destination of blockade runners operating from the British Isles led to the capture by the Federal navy of many of these ships.

The Quaker lawyer from New Jersey soon found himself engaged in a classic espionage duel with James Dunwoody Bulloch, a brilliant Confederate administrator who had been placed in charge of the South's Secret Service in the British Isles. Since the South had only a makeshift navy, Bulloch was determined to construct in British shipyards some of the most advanced naval vessels in the world.[18]

Palmerston's government, when declaring its proclamation of neutrality, had in a parallel step reinstated the British Foreign Enlistment Act of 1819. This legislation prohibited British subjects from enlistment in foreign armies or service and from "fitting out or equipping" vessels in the British dominion for war purposes without government approval. British subjects were forbidden to violate the lawful blockade of any nation at peace with England. The British were following the precedent set by President George Washington in his policy of neutrality during the war between England and France in 1793.[19]

Once Dudley had documented the Confederate shipbuilding program in Britain, he and Charles Francis Adams, the U.S. minister in London, began a long fight to get the Palmerston government to enforce its own law.

Within days of his arrival, Dudley discovered that a Confederate steam-powered gunboat named the *Oreto* was under construction in a Liverpool shipyard. He immediately sent exact descriptions and dimensions of the ship and proof of Confederate ownership to both Seward and Adams. Thus began a complex legal and diplomatic struggle to prevent the sailing of this Southern warship. Dudley and Adams became entangled in the arcane network of the British parliamentary and legal system involving various ministries, the law officers of the Crown, the lords commissioners of the Treasury who supervised the Customs Department, and finally, the customs collector at Liverpool who made final decisions on whether violations of the Foreign Enlistment Act had occurred. The customs collector proved to be a Confederate agent, and the *Oreto* was allowed to escape. It was clear that the Palmerston government would not go out of its way to enforce its own neutrality laws.

Bulloch sent his new warship out unarmed and under the command of a British captain and crew. When the *Oreto* arrived in the West Indies, the British Admiralty, under pressure from American authorities, seized the ship and brought it to trial under the Foreign Enlistment Act. The court determined that the ship was unarmed and that there was no evidence that it was intended to be used for hostile acts against the United States. As soon as the ship was released, it was armed, loaded with munitions, and renamed the *Florida,* and it set out on a long and successful cruise to destroy unarmed Northern merchant ships.

Soon after the escape of the *Oreto,* Dudley's spy operation uncovered another Confederate warship under construction in a Liverpool shipyard and began a second long duel with Bulloch to prevent its escape. After an intense legal and diplomatic struggle by Dudley and Adams to force the British to detain the new Confederate warship, Bulloch, taking advantage of the procrastination of British legal authorities and once again using clever stratagems, engineered the escape of what was to become the most famous Confederate warship in the American Civil War—the CSS *Alabama.*[20] Under the command of Raphael Semmes, a fanatical champion of slavery, the *Alabama,* together with its sister ship, the *Florida,* virtually destroyed the unarmed American merchant marine until both ships met their own fates in battles with Federal warships.

Although he failed to prevent the escape of the *Florida* and the *Alabama,* Consul Dudley uncovered all of Bulloch's ruses to get his warships out of Britain. Futhermore, he succeeded in placing his own spy aboard the *Alabama* and laid the groundwork for the British enforcement of its Foreign Enlistment Act against two more of the most formidable warships the Confederate navy had ever attempted to build in British shipyards. These soon became known to the world as the Laird Rams.

In July 1862, James Bulloch signed a contract with the Laird shipyard in Liverpool for the construction of two ironclad, steam-powered warships that would possess more armor and firepower than any Federal navy ship afloat. They were to be equipped with formidable underwater rams capable of sinking most wooden-hulled Federal warships. Bulloch's plan was to use these ships to break the Northern blockade, sail up the Potomac to threaten Washington, and then destroy the Federal navy yard at Portsmouth, New Hampshire. Thomas Dudley kept a close watch on the construction of the two rams and another screw steamer designed as a raider, the *Alexandra,* which was contracted to Confederate agents in Scotland. Soon he was able to send the exact dimensions of the new Southern warships to Seward and Adams.[21]

Dudley's espionage operation had completely infiltrated the Confederate network in the British Isles. No Confederate initiative was undertaken without his knowledge. One hundred years before the vast intelligence institutions of the modern world emerged, Dudley had mastered the arcana of covert operations. The Liverpool consul directed his network entirely independently from the London legation under Charles Francis Adams, who for diplomatic reasons did not wish to be involved with covert intelligence operations.

Thomas Dudley directed a counterintelligence watch on his own spies to ensure that they were not double agents for the Confederacy, often traveled incognito, prowled the docks and shipyards on his own, and was wary of Confederate disinformation schemes. At the same time, he used his consulate for open diplomatic and propaganda work with British officials and the public at large.

During the summer and fall of 1862, as the Confederacy rushed its program of naval construction in British shipyards, both England and France renewed their campaign for recognition of the South and active intervention in the war. With dwindling cotton supplies and the rise of mass unemployment in Britain's textile districts, the internal debate in the British cabinet and Parliament over recognition of the Confederacy reached a new height. After the defeat of the Union army at the second battle of Bull Run, both Palmerston and Russell believed the time to intervene had arrived. Chancellor of the Exchequer William Gladstone joined them.[22]

Lincoln, following Seward's advice, had waited for a major Union victory before announcing his Emancipation Proclamation.[23] The opportunity arrived with the bloody repulse of Lee's army at Antietam. In the following months, Lincoln's proclamation was instrumental in turning the tide of British public opinion in favor of the North. On the other hand, Foreign Minister Russell wrote a memorandum to his colleagues in the cabinet arguing that emancipation had simply given authority to the Union armies to commit "acts of plunder, incendiarism, and of revenge," actions that would bring about the destruction of the South.[24] Russell and other members of the British elite were terrified of a slave insurrection followed by a race war in America. The *Times* of London on October 7, 1862, wrote that Lincoln's Emancipation Proclamation would simply result in "horrible massacres of white women and children to be followed by the extermination of the black race in the South."[25]

Prime Minister Palmerston introduced a proposal from France for recognition of the Confederacy to his cabinet on November 11. He was supported in his motion to accept the French proposal for joint intervention in the war by Russell and Gladstone, but they were unable to capture a majority of the cabinet, and the proposal was turned down. Russell, informing the French of the rejection of their proposal for joint recognition, suggested that it be reconsidered in the spring, when the Democratic Party, which he believed opposed continuation of the war, would win a majority in the American Congress.[26] However, Adams and Dudley, who had conducted an intense diplomatic and public campaign against recognition of the Confederacy, could breathe a sigh of relief. Both had been prepared for a war with Britain and a break in diplomatic relations during the late fall of 1862.[27]

In the early months of 1863, when public opinion was turning in favor of the North, Dudley took every opportunity to participate in the propaganda war against Confederate sympathizers in England. He published his own pamphlets arguing the Northern cause and distributed them to every member of Parliament. In the meantime, the construction of the deadly new Confederate warships continued at top speed.

By uncovering the construction of the Laird Rams, Dudley's intelligence network alerted both the British and the American publics to the danger of continued violations of the Foreign Enlistment Act. The Northern public, seething over the piratical destruction of American merchant ships by the *Alabama* and *Florida,* expressed outrage over blockade runners from England pouring munitions into Southern ports and found it intolerable that Britain was now building ironclad ships for the Confederacy.

As a result of the depredations of the *Alabama* and *Florida* and the looming threat of the Laird Rams, Congress authorized the president to issue letters of marque as offical support for the creation of Northern privateers. The next day, March 3, Lincoln signed the new legislation permitting Union privateers, an act that was a direct threat to British shipping.[28]

A few weeks later, members of Lincoln's cabinet, including Secretary of the Treasury Salmon Chase and Secretary of the Navy Gideon Welles, put together a covert mission to Britain to build up Dudley's espionage operation. The Liverpool consul, who had been operating throughout the British Isles on a financial shoestring, was now about to get the full backing of Washington. This covert mission was headed by John Murray Forbes, a well-known business and political figure from Boston, and William Aspinwall, a prominent New York businessman and shipowner. The two emissaries were provided with $10 million in new government bonds to be used as security for a loan of £1 million by the Baring Brothers in London, which in turn would be used to purchase secretly any warship being built for the South in Britain. They were instructed to contact Thomas Dudley in Liverpool and Freeman Morse, the consul in London, for instructions on how this campaign might be carried out. Minister Adams was not informed of the real purpose of the Forbes-Aspinwall mission.

Forbes arrived in Liverpool on March 29, 1863, and immediately began lengthy discussions with Dudley on the consul's campaign to bring about the Crown seizure of the Laird Rams. Realizing that Dudley was not getting enough financial support for his covert operations in England, Forbes advanced him money to hire additional detectives and agents, and then wrote to Secretary of the Navy Welles pleading for more funds to support Dudley's network.

The scheme to secretly buy Southern warships under construction was made public by a leak to the London *Times,* which, in a detailed article, disclosed the real purpose of the visit to England by Forbes and Aspinwall. With secrecy lost, that mission was abandoned, and the two men devoted all their efforts to increasing Washington's support for Dudley's espionage operation. Two espionage jurisdictions were created, giving Dudley responsibility for Liverpool and northern England and Freeman Morse responsibility for London and the southern ports. However, Dudley remained the key station chief for Northern intelligence operations in the British Isles.[29]

As a result of Lincoln's Emancipation Proclamation, the propaganda war against the Confederacy by prominent American and British intellectuals, and the sympathy of the British working classes, with their traditonal hatred for slavery and support for free labor in the North, the public pressure on the Palmerston government to enforce neutrality laws against the Confederacy increased. On March 27, 1863, pro-Northern members of Parliament opened a debate on the Foreign Enlistment Act. William Forster blamed the government for allowing the *Alabama* to escape, called for amendments to tighten the act, and demanded that the Palmerston cabinet do everything in its power to maintain neutrality in the war.

Prime Minister Palmerston delivered an angry reply to these charges, claiming that the Federal government had no just cause for complaint. The prime minister labeled members of Parliament Forster, Richard Cobden, and John Bright as "the mouthpieces of the North."[30] Nevertheless, the Confederacy was losing its war for the public mind in Britain. After a complex legal struggle over Dudley's affidavits and depositions proving that the *Alexandria* was, in fact, a gunboat destined for the Confederate navy, the ship was detained by the Board of Customs on April 4. During this period, large public meetings called by the Emancipation Society and backed by British trade unions produced petitions to Parliament "to interpose its authority in order to prevent any more ships leaving England for the use of the Confederate States."[31] Dudley's covert operations had provided the ammunition for a public campaign.

By the summer of 1863, Northern military victories at Vicksburg and Gettysburg further undermined the Confederate cause in Britain. However, on the very day of the battle at Gettysburg, Dudley had learned that the first Confederate ram would be launched on July 4. Three days later, he made a formal application to the collector of customs, backed by extensive documentation, to detain what the consul considered to be the "most formidable and dangerous ships afloat." The Laird Rams set off the last great crisis of the American Civil War, threatening once again to bring about an armed conflict between London and Washington.

By the end of August, the Laird Rams were nearly completed and ready for launching. Lord Russell, after reviewing the voluminous documents on the rams prepared by Dudley and submitted to him by Adams, sent a reply on September 1 arguing that Dudley's evidence was simply hearsay; Confederate ownership had not been proven. The English government therefore found no grounds for detention. On September 5, Charles Francis Adams wrote his famous note to Russell declaring that if the British government allowed the rams to escape, "it would be superfluous in me to point out to your lordship that this is war."[32]

Dudley had joined Adams at his home in London to await Russell's answer. Both men now felt war was inevitable. When the new note from Palmerston's foreign minister arrived, it stated that the government still had the detention of the rams under consideration. Dudley observed that it looked as if the English government was backing down, and Adams agreed.[33]

The historical record shows that Russell had already determined to detain the rams and was searching for legal, political, and diplomatic means to resolve the crisis.[34]

After weeks of maneuvering by the Crown's highest legal authorities, Russell, under pressure of an imminent war with the United States and the immediate danger that the rams would escape, by his own authority ordered the seizure of the ram that was ready to sail on October 8. The cabinet approved his act after the fact. The second ram was later detained, and a few months later, both ships were purchased for use by the British Navy. The work of Thomas Dudley and Charles Francis Adams had, in effect, prevented the creation of a modern Confederate navy in British shipyards and as a result averted the final threat of war between Britain and the Union. Subsequent Union victories on the battlefield destroyed all Confederate hopes of foreign intervention.

While Seward, Dudley, and Adams were carrying on their diplomatic war against James Bulloch's rams, the *Florida* and *Alabama* continued to sweep the seas of American merchant ships. Finally, the *Alabama* was sunk in a historic sea battle by the USS *Kearsarge* off the coast of France on June 19, 1864. The *Florida* made its last attack at the end of September, and its cruise came to an end on October 4, 1864, when it was captured while at anchor in the Brazilian port of Bahia by the U.S. warship *Wachusett.* Confederate pirates had caused millions of dollars of damage to the Northern cause, but they could not win the war by themselves.

Other Confederate raiders disguised as merchant ships, namely the *Georgia* and the *Shenandoah,* were allowed to escape from the east coast of England during the final year of the American Civil War, but they could do little to affect the course of the war. Dudley was disgusted when the British courts and the House of Lords overturned on technical grounds the decision to detain the *Alexandria* and that ship, too, was released. Adams remarked to Dudley that the whole affair amounted to a legal comedy. However, Dudley succeeded in providing information that resulted in the detention in Scotland of two Confederate ironclad warships, the *Pampero* and the *Warrior.* James Bulloch, as early as February 1864, informed Stephen Russell Mallory, the head of the Confederate navy, that Dudley's spy network was making his own effort to create a modern Confederate navy in Britain impossible.

The American consul at Liverpool, through interviews with Northern captains of merchant ships sunk by the *Alabama* and *Florida,* together with other records he meticulously gathered over the years, built up massive and accurate files for claims made after the war by the U.S. government against Britain for its responsibility for U.S. war damages. These claims were presented to an international tribunal meeting in Geneva on December 15, 1871. Six months later, the British agreed to a settlement of the *Alabama* claims for $15.5 million to the United States as liability for the damage done by Confederate cruisers built in British shipyards.[35]

Although, in the final analysis, it was Union armies in the field that defeated the Confederate states, the struggle on the international front was crucial to that victory. A skillful combination of diplomacy, intelligence gathering, and mobilization of British public opinion led to the defeat of Confederate attempts to bring about foreign intervention in the American Civil War.

Historian Allan Nevins, speculating on the probable outcome of European intervention in America's Civil War, wrote: "Anglo-French intervention in the American conflict would probably have confirmed the splitting and consequent weakening of the United States; might have given French power in Mexico a long lease, with the ruin of the Monroe Doctrine, and would have led to the Northern conquest of Canada. The forces of political liberalism in the modern world would have received a disastrous setback."[36]

CHAPTER 1

The Second
American Revolution

AT FOUR-THIRTY IN THE MORNING OF APRIL 12, 1861, THE SOUTH OPENED the American Civil War by firing on Fort Sumter. A confrontation between two expanding societies had finally resulted in what a number of historians have referred to as the Second American Revolution. Southerners had made no secret of their grandiose fantasy of a slave empire extending from the American South through Mexico and Central America to the rim of South America, and then curving northward again through the West Indies to close the circle at Key West.[1]

It was the Southern design on the western states of Missouri, Kansas-Nebraska, New Mexico, and California, however, that brought about the collision with the equally expansive industrial and free labor market system of the North. The decade of the 1850s was marked by an accelerating crisis as the sectional antagonism between two opposing social systems developed into a hatred unrivaled in American politics. One Northern politician observed that "the people of the North and of the South have come to hate each other worse than the hatred between any two nations in the world."[2]

A common belief existed among Republican leaders that a victory of their party would lead to the gradual abolition of slavery through the admission of new free states into the Union and the eventual emancipation of slaves in the South. Moderate Republicans such as Abraham Lincoln, William Seward, and Charles Francis Adams understood clearly that the 1860 presidential election represented a watershed in the nation's history.

On the day of Lincoln's election, Charles Francis Adams, a leading New England abolitionist, wrote: "There is now scarcely a shadow of a doubt that the great revolution has actually taken place, and that the country has once and for all thrown off the domination of the slaveholders."[3] A few years earlier, William Seward, the national spokesman for the Republican Party, had declared: "I know, and you know, that a revolution has begun. I know and all the world knows, that revolutions never go backwards."[4] There was little doubt in anyone's mind, in either the North or the South, that the goal of this revolution was the end of slavery.

It was abundantly clear to Southern leaders that the new Republican Party's explicit platform in opposition to the extension of slavery was accompanied by an implicit determination to destroy the slave system wherever it existed. Delegates to the South Carolina secession convention, in a public proclamation, explained why they had seceded: "In spite of all disclaimers and professions, there can be but one end by the submission of the South to the rule of sectional anti-slavery government at Washington; and that end directly or indirectly, must be—the emancipation of the slaves of the South."[5] Alexander Stephens, the vice president of the Confederacy, declared that the cornerstone of the secessionist South rested upon the axiom that the black man was not equal to the white man; that slavery and subordination to the superior race was the black man's natural and moral condition.

Thus it came about that the revolution produced by Lincoln's election was met by a counterrevolutionary reaction of secession by Southern states and, within little more than a month after his inauguration, the launching of one of the most sanguinary wars in world history.

After his election, Lincoln put together a cabinet from the coalition of political forces that had elected him. The new president faced a chaotic and tumultuous situation at home and an uncertain response to the American crisis from Europe. The new president responded to the combined domestic and foreign crisis by naming his chief political rival, William Henry Seward, to the key post of secretary of state. With characteristic modesty, Lincoln confessed that he knew little about international relations and nothing about diplomacy. He informed Seward: "I shall have to depend upon you for taking care of the matters of foreign affairs of which I know so little, and with which I reckon you are so familiar."[6]

Lincoln's decision to make Seward the senior member of his cabinet and the subsequent contest between the two men for domination over the new administration have become a familiar part of the Lincoln legend. Seward delayed his acceptance of the nomination for three weeks, then attempted to force the promotion of his own candidates for key cabinet posts, but was in the end outmaneuvered by Lincoln. In the beginning, Seward did not believe that Lincoln was up to the presidency, but over time his disdain was transformed into profound respect and friendship.

As the senior member of the cabinet, Seward turned out to be a formidable, if at times volatile, statesman. He was described by William Howard Russell, the correspondent for the London *Times,* who himself was to play a controversial role in American affairs throughout the Civil War, as "a subtle, quick man rejoicing in power, given to peroration and to oracular utterances, fond of badinage, bursting with the importance of state mysteries, and with the dignity of directing the foreign policy of the greatest country—as all Americans think—in the world."[7] Seward, who had been a prominent politician for more than thirty years, was sixty years old at the time of his appointment as secretary of state. He had been elected governor of New York twice on the Whig ticket and had served since 1849 in the U.S. Senate, where he gained the reputation as the foremost Republican politician in the country.

One year before Lincoln's election, Seward had made a grand tour of Europe and been treated with great honor in Britain, where he was regarded as the next Republican candidate for president. According to one historian, Seward "was presented at Court and entertained by Lords Palmerston, Russell and Derby. Reveling in this flattering attention, he delayed his departure from England as long as he could and left with respect and kindness for all he had met." However, "the British had greeted him with more politeness than warmth. He had not impressed them personally and his career was not such that they would welcome his emergence as head of an American government."[8]

In fact, Prime Minister Palmerston and the British Foreign Office considered Seward to be hawkish and bellicose. Lord Lyons, the very able British minister to Washington, reporting to London on Seward's appointment, feared that the new secretary of state would unleash the Anglophobia of the American population and worried that Seward would simply use foreign policy as a tool to stir up popular opinion. The British minister had good grounds for these concerns, as Seward had once declared publicly that he considered Britain to be "the greatest, the most grasping and the most rapacious power" on earth.[9] The man who now held the second most powerful position in the nation had long stood for American domination of the continent, which, in his view, included control of Mexico, Central America, the Caribbean islands, and Canada. He was known in Britain and throughout the world as advocating a policy of utilizing war as "the best means of re-establishing internal peace."

After his appointment as secretary of state, Seward told William Howard Russell that to prevent British recognition of the Confederacy, he was prepared to go to war. The ultimate card Seward was ready to play against the British was the Northern threat to invade and annex Canada, and to encourage, aid, and abet rebellion in Ireland. During the election campaign, Seward had suggested that acquisition of Canada might compensate the Northern states for the loss of the South.

Once in office, Seward threatened that if London should in any way act as the patron of Southern privateers, the North would launch its own fleet of commerce raiders against British shipping. Whatever his threatening public statements, however, Seward proved to be capable of moderation and restraint, and in practice, he relied on international law and the British legal system as the main weapons for blunting Confederate operations in England. Nevertheless, England was always in doubt about possible Union actions. Lincoln's chief international statesman emerged as a formidable and astute diplomat who used both the carrot and the stick to achieve his goals, and his threat of war was most effective in causing the British to think twice before recognizing the Confederacy.

After his election, Lincoln had wished to pay a political debt to Gov. William Dayton of New Jersey by making him ambassador to England, but fortunately for American diplomacy, Seward intervened and claimed that position for his own political ally, Charles Francis Adams. The New England abolitionist was, like Seward, a nationally prominent Republican leader. He was the son of one former president and the grandson of another, each of whom had served as ambassador to London. Charles Francis Adams was a New England Brahmin and early abolitionist with a reputed private fortune of $2 million. It was said at the time that diplomacy ran in his blood and that he was the perfect choice for the London posting.

Adams had been a vice presidential nominee in 1848 and for a number of years had served as a prominent member of the House of Representatives. Lincoln acceded to Seward's request by appointing Charles Adams as minister to London and made William Dayton the ambassador to France. Charles Sumner, the powerful abolitionist from Massachusetts, opposed the appointment of Adams to London, hoping to obtain it for himself, but was appeased by his own subsequent selection for the powerful position as chairman of the Senate Committee on Foreign Relations.

Carl Schurz, a prominent German radical, a well-known journalist, and a man who was later to serve as one of Lincoln's army generals, gives us a vivid description of Charles Francis Adams. Stopping in at the London legation for a long visit with the new minister, Schurz describes Adams as a "little bald-headed gentleman with clean features and blue eyes," lacking personal charm or magnetism. "But his whole mental and moral being commanded so high a respect that every word he uttered had extraordinary weight, and in his diplomatic encounters his antagonists not only feared the reach and exactness of his knowledge and the solidity of his reasoning, but they were also anxious to keep his good opinion of them. He would not trifle with anything, and nobody could trifle with him."[10]

After that of minister, the next most important foreign affairs posting in Britain would subsequently turn out to be that of the consul at Liverpool, the major English seaport and center of Confederate operations in Britain. This appointment would go to Thomas Haines Dudley, an obscure Quaker lawyer from New Jersey. Dudley would provide the information on Confederate covert operations in Britain necessary for Seward and Adams to fight the diplomatic war against violations of British neutrality in the American Civil War. Given the isolation of the small American consulate in Liverpool, surrounded as it was by Confederate agents and their British sympathizers, Thomas Dudley was destined to face a lonely, arduous, complex, and dangerous assignment.

Thomas Haines Dudley was born in 1819 in Burlington County, New Jersey, heir to a long line of English Quakers who had established themselves in America in 1683 on his mother's side and in 1733 on his father's. Thomas Dudley's father died shortly after his birth, and Thomas, the youngest of four children, grew up working on his mother's farm. Dudley was reared in the tradition of English freeholders who helped mold the worldview of the Northern Atlantic states with the concept of free soil democracy that later emerged to confront the Southern slave system. The character of the man who was to become head of Lincoln's intelligence network in Britain was thus shaped by a generation of Northerners who created an ideology of antislavery.[11]

With hard-earned savings and the subsequent mortgaging of the family farm, Dudley studied law and was admitted to the bar in 1845. The young lawyer was an active Quaker, deeply involved in the emerging antislavery politics of the time. He took as his first case one that few young lawyers of his day had either the courage or the desire to undertake. It involved a free black family of Burlington County kidnapped by Southern slaveholders and forcibly returned to the South. Members of the Society of Friends of Burlington County had raised $1,000 to buy back the woman and her three children. Dudley knew the woman, who had once worked on his mother's farm, and took up the case with enthusiasm. He disguised himself as a slave trader in a broad-brimmed hat, purchased a whip, strapped on a pair of pistols, and pursued the kidnappers and their victims into the South, where his disguise allowed him to repurchase the woman and her children and return them to freedom.

On March 11, 1846, twenty-six-year-old Thomas Dudley married Emmaline Matlack in a Quaker ceremony in Camden. Two years later, established as a counselor at law, he was heavily engaged in state politics. His circle included a future Supreme Court justice, prominent officials in the state of New Jersey, and Henry C. Carey of Philadelphia, who was to become one of the most influential American economists of the nineteenth century. Carey and Dudley became close friends and maintained a lifelong correspondence concerning the protective tariff and other policies relating to American economic development. Both men reflected the optimism and pragmatic worldview of the expanding Northern industrial system and shared the New England belief that "bad roads meant bad morals." Both held the conviction that the one great threat to a prosperous economy, increasing social mobility, and the deepening of democratic institutions was the aggressive slavepower South.

By the mid-1850s, Thomas Dudley had been elected city treasurer of Camden, become the city solicitor, and was serving as chairman of the New Jersey executive committee of the new Republican Party. But at the height of this active period, Dudley experienced one of the most traumatic and fateful events of his life. On March 15, 1856, he was returning from business in Philadelphia on the ferry boat *New Jersey* when there was a terrible explosion. The headlines of the *New York Herald* told the story: "AWFUL CATASTROPHE ON THE DELAWARE; Burning of Philadelphia and Camden Ferryboat; TERRIBLE SCENE OF EXCITEMENT; THIRTY LIVES SUPPOSED TO BE LOST."[12]

Dudley, like the other passengers driven by the flames, threw off his overcoat, dove out as far as possible to escape the deadly paddlewheels, and surfaced among the ice floes on the river. From there, he saw passengers with their clothes on fire leaping into the freezing water. Overcome with cold, the New Jersey lawyer was finally pulled from the water by men in a small boat and then carried, apparently dead, to a hotel on the Camden shore. The initial efforts to bring him to life failed. But then, according to William Potts, an old friend of Dudley's who observed the riverboat disaster with thousands of other spectators on the New Jersey shore, "Mr. Albert S. Markley of Camden, a well-known director in the Camden & Amboy Railroad, happened in, recognized Dudley, and after long and persistent efforts, though told it was no use, the man was dead, restored him to consciousness."[13]

Although Dudley rarely referred to this experience, it had a profound and deleterious effect on his health and nervous system for the rest of his life. However, his resurrection from death had a major impact on American history, for Dudley was to play a pivotal role in the nomination of Abraham Lincoln for president.

At the age of forty, Thomas Dudley was one of the many Northern politicians who emerged to oppose the system of slavery. A tall man with a long face, steel gray eyes, and a Lincoln-style beard, Dudley combined stern principle with traditional Yankee practicality. Serious, often dour, he was nonetheless reported to be courteous and kind to both clients and colleagues, and was described by friend and foe alike as an indefatigable lawyer pursuing each case to its logical end. Despite chronic poor health brought on by his brush with death on the Delaware River, Dudley proved to be a man with an iron will. He represented the two main strands of Republicanism: the conservative view on protective tariffs and the radical strain of antislavery.

In 1860, Dudley served as chairman of the New Jersey executive committee of the Republican Party and was chosen as one of the delegates at large to represent his state at the Chicago Republican Convention. A newspaper correspondent wrote that the Chicago convention surpassed "all others, in enthusiasm, earnest of purpose, and fidelity to principle."[14]

The historian Allan Nevins argues that the Republican delegates were confident of victory in the national elections because of the split in the Democratic Party. "The growing freesoil enthusiasm of the North, the determination to resist the aggression of slavery, seemed a torrent suddenly bursting all barriers." Nevins describes the convention as:

> [the] first true people's convention in our annals; that is, the first in which the attendance and sentiment of the masses helped determine the result. . . . Until 1860 a limited hall sufficed for any convention and its visitors. But now the people pressed upon the scene. They descended on Chicago by the tens of thousands—thirty thousand in all; they crowded the railroads, steamboats, and highways; they filled the streets with bands and processions. They were full of optimism and crusading zeal. Chicago, realizing beforehand that no ordinary hall would do, had hastily provided the unique structure, the Wigwam, which comfortably held 10,000 people while 30,000 to 40,000 surged about the doors.[15]

At the time of the convention, William Seward, famous for his speech declaring the contest between North and South as an "irrepressible conflict," was the leading contender for the Republican presidential nomination. Abraham Lincoln of Illinois wrote to a friend six weeks before the convention: "My name is new in the field; and I suppose I am not the first choice of a very great many. Our policy, then is to give no offence to others—leave them in a mood to come to us, if they shall be impelled to give up their first love."[16]

Thomas Dudley and other New Jersey politicians were convinced that Seward, if nominated, could not be elected, and Dudley played the most prominent role in rallying New Jersey delegates behind the favorite-son candidacy of New Jersey's governor, William Dayton. The strategy was to hold the vote of the state for Governor Dayton until it could be cast for a winning candidate.

By the time of the convention, the Pennsylvania delegates were united behind their own governor, Simon Cameron, while Illinois and Indiana supported Lincoln. As one observer commented: "It was narrowed down to this; the four doubtful states must unite upon a candidate or Seward would be nominated."[17] In the meantime, Massachusetts and the other New England states had informed the delegates from New Jersey, Pennsylvania, Indiana, and Illinois that if they could not agree on a candidate, the New England states would vote for Seward.

The convention opened on Wednesday, and Dudley, who had been assigned to the platform committee, was occupied with writing the plank on protective tariffs. On Thursday, the delegates from the four pivotal states met at Cameron Hall to attempt to unite behind one candidate. A participant later recalled the meeting: "Ex Governor Reeder presided. It was a noisy assemblage, and it very soon became evident that nothing could be accomplished as affairs then stood. Mr. Dudley then proposed to Mr. Judd, of Illinois, that the matter should be referred to a committee of three from each of the four states."

Thomas Dudley made the motion, it was carried, and the committee adjourned to the room of David Wilmot, the Pennsylvania delegate who had gained fame in the House for framing the Wilmot Proviso, a statement declaring that slavery should forever be prohibited in a territory acquired from Mexico. The committee remained in session from six to ten o'clock in the evening without reaching an agreement. The delegates from each state attempted to convince the others that only their own candidate was the best qualified. Horace Greeley, editor of the *New York Tribune,* knocked on the door and was admitted to the meeting. After being told that a stalemate existed, Greeley left the room and telegraphed the *Tribune* that William H. Seward would be nominated the next day on the second ballot. The *Tribune* printed the telegram on Friday.

A journalist who had access to the proceedings described the events that followed and Thomas Haines Dudley's role in breaking the stalemate, preventing the nomination of Seward, and assuring Lincoln's subsequent victory: "Finding that the committee was about to separate without achieving any result, Mr. Dudley took the floor, and proposed that it should be ascertained which one of the three candidates had the greatest actual strength before the convention, and could carry the greatest number of delegates from the four states in the event of dropping the other two."[18]

After a detailed analysis, state by state, it was determined that Lincoln was the strongest candidate. Dudley then proposed to the Pennsylvania delegates that for the good of the party, they should give up their candidate and unite behind Lincoln. After more discussion, Dudley's proposal was adopted. A strategy was devised that Governor Dayton would receive one or more complimentary favorite-son votes, and then the delegates would be thrown behind Lincoln. The Pennsylvania delegation would follow the same pattern, voting first for Cameron and then for Lincoln. The agreement among the four pivotal states had not been generally known when the convention assembled.

It therefore came as a bombshell when Thomas Haines Dudley of New Jersey, on the third ballot, rose and cast his vote for Lincoln. All the other delegates from New Jersey, except one, followed Dudley's endorsement of Lincoln; the Pennsylvania delegation joined the Lincoln bandwagon, the New England states carried out their promise to support any unanimous candidate agreed upon by the four doubtful states, and Lincoln was nominated. The journalist summed up the role played by Thomas Dudley in this historic event:

> It was the action of the committee from the four doubtful States which undoubtedly secured Mr. Lincoln's nomination; but for this Mr. Seward would have been nominated, and there is little doubt, just as surely defeated. This is the plain narrative of the manner in which the nomination of Abraham Lincoln was brought about. It cannot be disguised that, had it not been for Mr. Dudley's energy and tact in the committee of the doubtful states, the nation in the emergency which so soon followed would not have had the service of that great and good man at the helm.[19]

Soon after the nomination, in a letter to Lincoln, Dudley wrote:

> Our people pretty generally think the day for compromise and concession has gone by and that our true policy is to stand by the platform laid down at Chicago; let the consequences be what they may. . . . In my judgement, the only way to settle the slavery question effectually is to stand firm to our principles and resist the further extension. If the South goes out of the Union let her go; she can never dissolve this union with less cause to justify it or when we stand upon firmer ground to resist it.[20]

Lincoln, the astute politician, co-opted his principal rival, William Seward, by making him secretary of state, paid his debt to Governor Dayton by making him minister to France, and gave Charles Francis Adams the key post in London. Adams arrived in London on May 14, 1861, with his wife, Abigail; his fifteen-year-old daughter, Mary; and his two sons, Henry, age twenty-three, and Brooks, twelve. The new U.S. minister was presented to the queen by Prime Minister Palmerston on the sixteenth.

At about the same time, Thomas Dudley traveled to Europe seeking medical treatment and stayed in Paris to help his friend William Dayton establish the U.S. mission in France. Then, on June 24, Dudley paid a visit to Adams at the London legation. Benjamin Moran, the acerbic secretary of the U.S. legation in London, who kept a secret diary during the war, described Dudley in his journal:

> He has a fine head and remarkably intellectual countenance. His hair is dark brown and wavy and sets off his high and broad forehead with great effect, altho' at the same time concealing much of it. He is as intelligent as he looks and talks with great force. . . . I was much gratified to find him a strenuous patriot. He is modest, refined and able and would make a splendid European representative. I should say he was 42 years of age, has a genteel figure, and is fully 6 feet high.[21]

During Dudley's absence, political figures from the Eastern states reminded Lincoln of the role played by Thomas Dudley at the Chicago convention, and on his return to the United States, Dudley was summoned to the White House by Lincoln. Recalling the meeting at a later time, Dudley states that he sought a foreign appointment for health reasons.

> When I applied to the President he looked at me and said, Mr. Dudley there are but two places that are worthy of your acceptance that have not already been filled; one is the consulship at Liverpool, the other Minister to Japan. If you desire it I will have a commission made out for you as Minister to Japan. I replied, Mr. President, I am sick and stand in need of good medical advice, I could not get that in Japan, but could at Liverpool, therefore I would rather take the subordinate position of Consul at Liverpool than Minister to Japan.[22]

Lincoln had wanted to reserve the consulship at Liverpool for his friend Gustave Koerner, the powerful leader of the German Republican faction in

Illinois, but when Koerner took the post as minister to Spain, Lincoln appointed Dudley to the Liverpool position. Thus, almost by accident, Thomas Dudley would play the role in Civil War diplomacy that history had assigned him.

When he was called in for his final meeting with Lincoln, Dudley recalls, the president "went to his table and wrote a note to the Secretary of State which he read to me in the following language, 'You will please make out a commission for my friend Thomas Dudley of New Jersey as United States Consul at Liverpool.' He sent the note by one of his messengers to the secretary's office. I thanked him for it, took him by the hand to bid him farewell telling him I thought I should return home in about a year's time. This was the last time I ever saw Abraham Lincoln."[23] In fact, the New Jersey lawyer would spend more than ten years at his post. Liverpool had long been the most important seaport in Britain. The American consulate at Liverpool was a position that had been occupied by a number of illustrious predecessors, including Nathaniel Hawthorne.

Dudley would soon join Seward and Adams in the diplomatic and intelligence war against the Confederacy abroad. Dudley's position in the diplomatic hierarchy, to put it in the language of our own time, was equivalent to that of station chief of intelligence operations in Britain. In this role, the Quaker lawyer from New Jersey proved to be the main obstacle to the construction of a powerful steam-powered Confederate navy built in British shipyards.

CHAPTER 2

The Balance of Power

FOR BOTH NORTH AND SOUTH, THE STRATEGIC STAKES IN THE DIPLOMATIC struggle to win British support were enormous and potentially decisive for the outcome of the Civil War. For the South, British recognition of the Confederacy was a major war aim. Victory was assured, Southern leaders believed, once Great Britain granted recognition to the new sovereign power in Richmond and then intervened with her navy to break the Northern blockade of Southern ports. Because of British dependence on the South's cotton, Southern leaders argued that the logic of recognition appeared irrefutable. E. J. Hobsbawm, the British historian, clearly defines the historic relationship between Britain and the American Southern states: "Thus the American Civil War, whatever its political origins, was the triumph of the industrialized North over the agrarian South, almost, one might say, the transfer of the South from the informal empire of Britain (to whose cotton industry it was the economic pendant) into the new major industrial economy of the United States."[1]

The doctrine of "king cotton diplomacy" was spelled out in the U.S. Senate by Sen. Louis Wigfall of Texas on December 12, 1860: "I say that cotton is King, and that he waves his sceptre not only over these thirty-three states, but over the island of Great Britain and over continental Europe, and that there is no crowned head upon that island, or upon the continent that does not bend the knee in fealty and acknowledge allegiance to that monarch."[2] In short, the South's military and diplomatic fortunes were staked on the belief that England, defined by textiles, was dependent on the South for her livelihood. The North's passage of the Morill Protective Tariff Act, directed at English imports, appeared to confirm the Southern conviction that British interests dictated recognition of the Confederacy. Thus the threat of foreign intervention on the side of the South would haunt Washington for the duration of the war.

Southern leaders were naturally delighted when very early in the war, William Gregory, a member of Parliament, introduced a motion calling for Britain's recognition of the Confederacy. They were further encouraged when England's foreign minister, Lord John Russell, gave a noncommittal reply to an official request from Washington that Britain neither grant recognition to the Confederacy nor encourage any hopes of recognition.

Seward, Adams, and Dudley were to confront formidable and experienced statesmen in their long duel with the British government. Henry John Temple, Lord Palmerston, who had served in successive British governments for over fifty years, was seventy-six years old when the American Civil War broke out. Holding the office of both foreign minister and head of government, Palmerston had won fame for his skill at the balance-of-power game among the great powers. An unswerving nationalist, he pursued imperial aims by proclaiming that England had no permanent friends nor permanent enemies, only permanent interests. Richard Cobden, an outstanding friend of the American North in the British Parliament, once remarked that the prime minister liked to drive the wheel close to the edge and show how dexterously he could avoid falling over the precipice. Washington and London would repeatedly come dangerously close to the precipice of war in the years between 1861 and 1865.

Palmerston had contempt for American democracy and considered the United States to be inherently aggressive, a characteristic he believed needed to be checked by superior power. He was hardly displeased by the troubles in North America and even evinced some pleasure at what he termed the new "disunited States of America." Palmerston belonged to that sector of the British elite that had little sympathy for either side of the conflict in America. In this view, since Britain itself had abolished the slave trade in 1833 and the Lincoln administration had done little as yet to do so, the war appeared simply to be a struggle between two centers of power. The British were mainly concerned with the possible interruption of their own profitable commerce with the North American continent.

Lord John Russell's distinguished career rivaled that of Palmerston; he too had served both as prime minister and foreign minister. The two men depended upon each other as either competitors or allies. Russell was small, shy, frail, and reclusive. He lacked the power and polish of Palmerston and served in his shadow. It was clear that Palmerston had the final word in the making of British policy, although Russell was in charge of American affairs and paid a great deal of attention to them.

On May 2, 1861, Lord Russell announced to the British Parliament that "nothing but the imperative duty of protecting British interests if they should be attacked justifies the government in intervening" in the American conflict. "We have not been involved in any way in that contest by any act or giving any advice in the matter, and for God's sake, let us if possible keep out of it."[3] The next day, however, Russell held an informal discussion with three Confederate commissioners who had just arrived in England. This meeting was denounced by newspapers in the North as the first step in British recognition of the South as a sovereign state. Secretary of State Seward expressed outrage at the "duplicity and arrogance" of British leaders and was determined not to tolerate this state of affairs. He told Senator Sumner, "God damn them, I'll give them hell."[4]

In the ensuing debate in Parliament, Lord Russell, answering a question from William Gregory, the Confederate sympathizer, replied that "the Southern Confederate states must be recognized by Great Britain as belligerents." After further discussion, the British Parliament on May 13 issued a proclamation of neutrality based on the Foreign Enlistment Act. This old law prohibited British subjects from enlisting in a foreign conflict and from equipping ships of war for either side in America. The proclamation ordered that any vessel equipped for war in a British port be confiscated. Violators, at least in theory, faced punishment in British courts. It was this legal ruling that Thomas Dudley and Charles Francis Adams would attempt to use in their struggle to prevent the building of Confederate warships in British shipyards. However, the law covering the construction of warships was vague in detail, and Confederate agents were quick to take advantage of British reluctance to enforce their proclaimed policy of neutrality.

At the same time, the British government took steps to reinforce the defense of Canada and made it clear that both North and South would be treated equally as belligerents in a common conflict. Both would be subject to international law according to the rules of the Treaty of Paris of 1856. Those rules declared that for a blockade to be honored, it must be proved effective, and no neutral power would be required to recognize a paper blockade, meaning a simple declaration of blockade without the ability to enforce it.

The British Proclamation of Neutrality followed shortly after Lord Russell's meeting with the Confederate commissioners and just one day before the arrival of Charles Adams, the U.S. minister to London. Adams seemed to be faced with a *fait accompli* before he had even taken up his post. Britain had recognized the South on equal terms as a belligerent; thus the Confederacy appeared to be only one step away from winning diplomatic recognition as a sovereign nation.

Seward put his "give them hell" threat into effect by sending a dispatch to Adams threatening war with Britain if London dared to recognize the Confederacy. He wrote that if Britain should give official recognition to the South, "we from that hour, shall cease to be friends and become once more as we have twice before been forced to be, enemies of Great Britain."[5] Lincoln, after reading Seward's dispatch, is reported to have replied, "One war at a time!" The president ordered Seward to tone down the language of the dispatch and to give Adams a good deal of discretion for a verbal deliverance of the message. When Adams met with Russell, he softened Seward's words while retaining the gravity of their content. The urbane Lord Russell assured the American minister that Britain had no present intention of granting recognition to the Confederacy and that he "had no expectation of seeing them any more."[6] He kept his word and refused to meet with Southern envoys again. Nevertheless, British intervention in the American war continued to rest solely on whether it was perceived to be in the interests of Great Britain.

It would be six months from the time Adams arrived in London to the day when Thomas Haines Dudley took up his consular duties in Liverpool. During that time, the war went badly for the North, which had yet to prove its ability to subdue Southern armies and prevent the permanent establishment of a sovereign Confederate state. England and France were acting in concert to enforce their stated policies of neutrality and in the effort to treat both North and South equally as belligerents in a common war. A strenuous effort by Seward to divide the two European powers had failed, and the blockade of Southern ports was sporadic and only partially effective. At the same time, a voluntary Southern embargo of cotton exports had reduced supplies for the British textile industry and threatened England with mass unemployment.

The British cabinet distrusted Lincoln's government, and British public opinion was in the main hostile to the North, in particular because the Northern states refused to come out unconditionally against slavery. British antagonism toward Washington was matched by the hostility toward Britain of the Northern population and its representatives in Congress. During the first year of the war, Britain had quietly strengthened its North American squadron of warships and reinforced Canadian garrisons. For its part, the South had failed to win recognition from London and realized that any successful diplomatic strategy rested upon victories on the battlefield and the hope that dwindling British cotton supplies would force Britain to intervene in order to break the Northern blockade of Southern coasts. Southern hopes were encouraged by early military victories over disorganized Union armies.

By the fall of 1861, Charles Francis Adams was despondent over the humiliating Northern defeat at the first battle of Bull Run. The London

Times correspondent William Howard Russell, who had witnessed the battle, described the collapse of the Union forces and their pell-mell retreat as a "miserable, ceaseless panic." Adams had become convinced that "as a whole the English are pleased with our misfortunes" and that they held a general opinion of the United States that was "unfriendly and jealous."[7] Confirming his view was a speech delivered by Lord Russell at Newcastle, where he declared that the American Civil War was simply a conflict between one side fighting for empire and the other for power. In the same speech, Russell implied that the Continental powers might take some action to end the "sanguinary conflict" in America.

What Russell had in mind was spelled out in a letter to Palmerston. Russell suggested an Anglo-French declaration to both North and South, telling the belligerents to "make up your quarrels; we propose to you terms of pacification which we think fair and equitable. If you accept them, well and good; but if your adversary accepts them and you refuse them our mediation is at an end, and you may expect to see us as your enemies."[8] Russell argued that Britain should wait before issuing such a declaration until February of the following year, when cotton supplies would be running low in the textile districts and the conservative opposition would be clamoring for intervention in the North American conflict. There was little question that bankrupt mill owners and tens of thousands of unemployed workers posed a threat to any British government.

Prime Minister Palmerston rejected Russell's plan for intervention in the war on the grounds that he did not wish to risk war with Washington at that time. He believed the North would be unable to maintain its blockade during the winter months, while the British would have similar difficulty supplying Canada. Palmerston furthermore distrusted the French, who might desert their English allies once engaged in a war with America and follow a course of aggressive expansion in Europe. "The only thing to do," Palmerston told Russell, "seems to be to lie on our oars and to give no pretext to the Washingtonians to quarrel with us, while on the other hand we maintain our rights and those of our fellow countrymen."[9] The British thus decided to watch and wait and gauge their actions by the course of the war itself. Despite this caution, the risk of war between the two powers, particularly through accident or blunder, remained high.

Such a blunder occurred at the very time Thomas Haines Dudley was in midocean on his way to Liverpool. Dudley sailed with his family from New York aboard the steamer *Africa* on November 6, 1861. On the eighth, Capt. Charles Wilkes, commander of the American warship *San Jacinto,* fired a shot across the bow of the British mail steamer *Trent* as it crossed through the

Bahama Channel. The *Trent* was carrying two high-level Confederate diplomats, James Mason and John Slidell. The Union captain, acting without orders from Washington, was determined to capture them.

Wilkes, an impulsive and ambitious naval commander, was known for his skill as an explorer and navigator. After studying international law on the seizure of neutral ships carrying contraband goods, Wilkes, seeking to make a name for himself, stopped the *Trent*. He then sent two boats carrying a boarding party of twenty men armed with cutlasses and pistols, led by Lt. D. M. Fairfax, the executive officer of the *San Jacinto*. Fairfax had orders to seize the ship's papers, passenger lists, the two Southern diplomats, and their secretaries.

Mason and Slidell hurriedly gave their dispatch bag to the captain, who locked up the papers in the ship's mailroom. Norman Ferris, in his history of the *Trent* affair, records the scene as it unfolded:

> Instructing his boat crew to remain seated and quietly to await further orders, Fairfax climbed to the *Trent*'s main deck, where an indignant Captain James Moir awaited him. A hostile crowd of seventy or eighty passengers and crewmen, edged forward to listen. Upon being introduced to Moir, the American Lieutenant said that he had been informed that enemies of the United States named Mason and Slidell were on board the *Trent*. He asked to see her passenger list. Hearing his name mentioned, a paunchy, white-haired gentleman stepped toward Fairfax and certified himself as Slidell. Soon the thin-lipped, red-nosed Mason joined the group. . . . Fairfax then announced that he had orders "to arrest Mr. Mason and Mr. Slidell and their secretaries, and send them to the United States war vessel nearby."[10]

The passengers began shouting, "Throw the damned fellow overboard!" Seeing their officer threatened, the armed sailors waiting in the boats rushed aboard, flourishing their weapons. Slidell's wife and daughter threw themselves into the fray by berating Fairfax and his sailors. But in short order, Mason and Slidell were forcibly escorted down the side of the ship as prisoners, accompanied by the hysterical screams of Slidell's daughter and shouts of "pirates" by the passengers. The British commander "loudly threatened that the British Navy would retaliate within a few weeks by destroying the entire Northern blockade."[11]

Two weeks later, the *San Jacinto* anchored in Boston Harbor, where Mason and Slidell were imprisoned at Fort Warren. Wilkes immediately became a national hero at a time of Northern defeats. Congress passed a strong resolution congratulating Wilkes on his heroic exploit, and crowds of cheering citizens gathered to greet him wherever he went. Gideon Welles, U.S. secretary of the navy, wrote a congratulatory letter to Wilkes, which was then published by Northern newspapers. However, the *Trent* affair was clearly a violation of international law and brought the Union to the brink of war with Britain. Dudley's mission was in danger of ending before it had begun.

Dudley arrived in Liverpool on the nineteenth of November, during the height of the *Trent* crisis. He and his family were met at the dock by a messenger from the consulate, and then taken by horse cabs to Mrs. Blodget's boarding house at 153 Duke Street, where rooms had been engaged for them.

Liverpool was Britain's main port of entry for cotton from the American South and had grown rich on the slave trade in the eighteenth and early nineteenth centuries. The port of Liverpool stretched for five miles along the Mersey River. Herman Melville had described the sprawling docks and teeming city in his autobiographical novel *Redburn,* written in the 1840s:

> I beheld long China walls of masonry; vast piers of stone; and a succession of granite-rimmed docks; completely enclosed, and many of them communicating, which almost recalled to mind the great American chain of lakes: Ontario, Erie, St. Clair, Huron, Michigan and Superior. The extent and solidity of these structures, seemed equal to what I had read of the old pyramids of Egypt. . . . In magnitude, cost and durability, the docks of Liverpool, even at the present day surpass all others in the world.[12]

The port, in addition, possessed the most modern shipyards in the world capable of building the newest ironclad, steam-powered ships. It was here that the South had determined to construct a modern navy.

By the time of Dudley's arrival, Liverpool had become a stronghold of Confederate sympathizers. Benjamin Moran, the secretary of the American mission in London, lost no time in informing Dudley that Liverpool was swarming with Confederate agents. The port, Moran wrote, was simply "a nest of pirates"[13] who were energetically engaged in establishing this great English seaport and industrial center as a base for the purchase of munitions for the Southern armies and the creation of a Confederate navy in British shipyards.

Before Thomas Dudley's arrival, the American consulate in Liverpool had been in the hands of a very capable acting consul, Henry Wilding. A British-born American possessing an expert knowledge of the commercial and organizational life of Liverpool, Wilding had kept a careful eye on Confederate activities in the port. Dudley readily retained the services of Wilding, appointing him vice consul, and the two men worked as a team to put together a formidable intelligence network targeted against covert Confederate operations in Britain.

A short time after his arrival, the new consul was paid a formal visit by twenty Liverpool businessmen who were members of the Chamber of Commerce. Thomas Dudley faced for the first time the atmosphere of hostility produced by the *Trent* affair and the sympathy for the South that existed among all classes of Liverpool society. Dudley recalls that "a feeling prevailed there that it was impossible for the North ever to suppress the rebellion," and that the only way to achieve it "was to permit the South to sever the union."[14] English trade was seriously affected by the war, and the newspapers of England asserted that the rebellion could never be suppressed. According to Dudley, the great mass of the people and the most influential men of Liverpool all believed the South would soon emerge as a sovereign nation.

After Wilding had introduced the businessmen of Liverpool to Consul Dudley, a Mr. Melby, who was secretary of the board of the Liverpool association, made a formal address. After giving Dudley a cordial welcome, he launched into a criticism of the actions of the U.S. government in attempting to crush the rebellion. Dudley recalls that "the thought immediately came to me that it was necessary for me to be very decided in my reply."

When it was his turn to speak, the consul countered the criticism of the Union by replying that "the nature of the conflict grew out of slavery, the question involved was whether human slavery should be limited and confined to the South or should expand into a slave empire." Dudley went on to say that he was already aware of "the feeling existing in England of the impossibility of the Government to suppress the rebellion." He then stated that it made little difference whether many people in England believed that the rebellion "should not be suppressed but succeed in the formation of a separate and distinct government in the South," or thought it had come into being "from the inability of the government of the U.S. to suppress it." With great emotion, the Quaker lawyer described the antislavery cause to which he was dedicated:

> You would tell me that history did not furnish any example of any rebellion ever having been suppressed that had assumed the gigantic proportions of this rebellion. . . . But you must bear in mind that this rebellion is different in its character from any of those which history gives to us. Those rebellions were against oppression, it was the people rebelling against their oppressors—liberty against tyranny. This rebellion in the U.S. is not such, it is the reverse, it is the oppressors rebelling against liberty, it is a rebellion got up in favor of slavery against liberty, for the purpose of perpetuating human slavery. . . . It is

to destroy the best, finest and freest government that the sun shines upon . . . to build upon its ruins an immense slave empire—to hold people in perpetual bondage. Notwithstanding the gigantic proportions it has assumed and the moral aid and assistance it may have received in this and other European countries or the aid it may hereafter receive from you or them, just as sure as there is a righteous God in Heaven, this rebellion will not succeed.

Dudley concluded his peroration with some advice to his audience: "Do not deceive yourselves—the rebellion will be put down, the Government of the U.S. intends to suppress it if it takes the shedding of the last drop of human blood and the expenditure of the last dollar in the treasury." As the Liverpool businessmen left, Dudley recalls that he observed that his remarks had not been expected and had left an unfavorable impression on his visitors.[15] However, his audience must have realized that Confederate sympathizers in Britain now had a formidable adversary.

First reports of the forcible boarding of the British mail steamer *Trent* reached London on November 27. There were few who did not realize the gravity of the situation, and Palmerston called a cabinet meeting on the twenty-ninth. At that meeting, it was agreed that the boarding of the *Trent* had been a violation of international law and the rights of Great Britain, and the British government expected an apology and the immediate release of the prisoners, who would be turned over to Britain. If these demands were refused, Britain would break diplomatic relations with Washington and recall its minister. The cabinet met again on the thirtieth and reaffirmed the decision to demand that the United States return the Confederate envoys with an apology for their capture. After receiving these demands, the United States was to be given seven days for a reply before the British recalled their own envoy from Washington. In the meantime, London began preparations for war with the United States.[16]

Russell and Palmerston called for a ban on the export of saltpeter to the United States, a serious blow to the North, since England was the only source of supply for this ingredient essential for explosives. In addition, Washington was prohibited from purchasing all other types of munitions and military materials. The Admiralty sent three battleships, two frigates, and a corvette to Adm. Alexander Milne to reinforce his North Atlantic squadron, and fifteen more ships were readied for commission. On December 3, Palmerston, Russell, and their military advisors agreed to send 10,500 troops as reinforcements for North America. The Canadians immediately called up reserves and prepared for the war they now believed likely.[17]

The most bellicose British newspapers proclaimed that England had been "piratically outraged" and that the insult to the British flag "must not go unavenged." The more sober London *Times* argued that it was not the duty of a ship's captain to decide cases of international law on his own. "The legal course would have been to take the ship itself into port and to ask for her condemnation, or for the condemnation of the passengers, in a Court of Admiralty." The less measured comment of the London *News* labeled the *Trent* seizure as "wanton folly" by an "imbecile" government at Washington. The *News* demanded that the Americans "disavow the act, restore Messrs. Mason and Slidell, and tender the fullest apology. Nothing short of this reparation can be accepted."[18]

On Christmas Day 1861, Secretary Seward heard from William Dayton in France that the *Trent* affair had caused an uproar in Paris, and that the crisis would "require the most delicate handling or it will be followed by consequences which every patriot must deplore." Thurlow Weed, one of Seward's closest political associates, who had been sent to Europe on a special mission to counter Confederate propaganda, warned of an inevitable war should the United States uphold the *Trent* seizure. Both Weed and Charles Francis Adams reported on the feverish war preparations in England. Adams noted that in England, there was "an almost universal demand for satisfaction for the insult and injury thought to be endured by the action of Captain Wilkes." He added that "a collision is inevitable" if the U.S. government backed Wilkes. "My present expectation is that by the middle of January at farthest, diplomatic relations will have been sundered between the two countries."[19] Richard Cobden, who openly supported the Northern cause in Parliament, wrote to his friend Senator Sumner that France would support England in whatever action it chose to pursue and warned Sumner to take this into account.

These dire warnings from abroad had a decided effect on the debate in Lincoln's cabinet over the *Trent* affair. A majority of the cabinet soon expressed a desire to avoid war with England. Lincoln, who, early in the crisis, had supported international arbitration of the dispute, gave up that position in favor of a more direct action to avoid war with England.

Attorney General Edward Bates expressed the growing consensus of the men around Lincoln when he stated: "In such a crisis, with such a civil war upon our hands, we cannot hope for success in a war with England, backed by the assent and countenance of France. We must evade it—with as little damage to our honor and pride as possible."[20] According to the historian Norman Ferris, only Seward understood a way out of the crisis. It was Charles Francis Adams "who furnished the Secretary of State with the crucial ingredient in his argument" for a diplomatic solution to the crisis.[21]

Writing to Seward on December 3, Adams suggested that Washington take up the traditional American stand on neutral nations and the freedom of their ships from search first advanced by Madison in 1804. Adams argued that "our neutral rights are as valuable to us as ever they were, whilst time has reflected nothing but credit on our steady defence of them against superior power." Although England demanded neutral rights for its own merchant ships, the American doctrine of neutral rights had, in fact, never been honored by the British fleet. Seward, taking Adams's advice, was able to fashion a reply to the British based on traditional American principles of the rights of neutral ships at sea. Madison had written that "whenever property found in a neutral vessel is supposed to be liable on any ground to capture and condemnation, the rule in all cases is that the question shall not be decided by the captor but be carried before a legal tribunal where a regular trial may be had, and where the captor himself is liable for damages for an abuse of power."[22]

Another historian, Brian Jenkins, argues that the Lincoln administration "was saved from domestic reproach by Seward. His despatch was a masterpiece of its kind. Seward argued that Wilkes had acted on his own authority but not improperly. His one error had been his failure to take the vessel in as a prize. The officer's reasons were given and his oversight described as an act of prudence and generosity."[23] Seward's dispatch defused the crisis. Mason and Slidell were put aboard a British warship in January. The secretary of state had complied with British demands and yet made the whole affair acceptable to the American people, who felt that national honor had been maintained.

In the last year of his life, Thomas Dudley provided an interesting historical footnote to the *Trent* affair in an account written for a scholarly journal. Dudley states that according to information he received at the time, it was Queen Victoria and Prince Albert who played a key role during the *Trent* crisis in preventing war between England and America. Dudley's account, although based on secondhand information, has been confirmed by the historical record.

Dudley reveals that Lord Russell had written an

offensive despatch, addressed to our government, complaining of the seizure, and demanding the surrender of Mason and Slidell. This despatch was written as an excuse for the war which they intended to declare, and was couched in such language as to bring it about. If this despatch had been sent in the way it was written it would undoubtedly have precipitated a war between the two countries. We would never have afforded to surrender Mason and Slidell at the dictation of such a despatch. Our government would never have done it. Our dignity and self-respect as a nation would not have permitted us to do so. That England at that time intended war with us cannot be doubted.

Dudley then recalls the celebrated cartoon published at the time of Britannia resting her elbow on a loaded cannon, pointing toward the United States, with the inscription below it: "Waiting for an Answer!"[24]

Dudley goes on to outline the extensive preparations for war undertaken by the English government at the time of the *Trent* crisis, and finally describes the role played by Queen Victoria and Prince Albert. According to Dudley, Russell's warlike dispatch was taken to the queen for her approval.

It was placed in her hands while she was sitting at the bedside of her sick husband, the Prince Consort. She betrayed emotion while reading it, which was observed by the Prince. He turned and asked her what it was that so disturbed her. She told him, and expressed her displeasure at the language and the tone of the despatch. He asked to see it. It was handed to him, and after he had read it over he remarked, "This will never do; it must not be sent in this form; it is couched in offensive language, such as will irritate and provoke a war between the two nations." He asked for a pencil, and they propped him up in bed; he took the pencil and went through the despatch, striking out the offensive and harsh language, and interlined it so as to modify and tone it down.[25]

The message was sent as rewritten by Prince Albert, and Dudley argues that as a result of its respectful tone, Mason and Slidell were released and war was avoided. Dudley concludes his description of these events with the comment that the return dispatch "written by Mr. Seward was probably the most able state paper he ever wrote."

Dudley reveals that he learned the inside story of the intervention by Queen Victoria and Prince Albert in the *Trent* affair while visiting his friend William Dayton at the Paris Embassy. He writes that one morning, Dayton received a letter from Lord Cowley, the British minister to France, "requesting him to call on Lady Cowley during the day, stating she was anxious to see him. He showed me the letter expressing curiosity to the cause of its being written." While Dudley waited at the American mission, Dayton drove off in a carriage to the British legation. Lady Cowley, who was a very close friend of the queen, told Dayton the story of how the prince consort had altered the British dispatch to Washington on the *Trent* affair. The queen wished Americans to know the facts in the case and requested that Lady Cowley communicate them to the American minister in Paris. On his return from the British legation in Paris, Judge Dayton told Dudley the whole story and "wrote the same to the State Department in Washington." British and American historians support Dudley's version of this event. The prince consort died of typhoid fever on December 14, 1861. It is clear that the rewriting of the *Trent* dispatch was the last important act of his life.

London received news of the release of Mason and Slidell on January 8, 1862, and the immediate crisis was resolved. The British press congratulated the country for teaching the Americans that it was "unsafe to presume upon British patience too far" and concluded that the United States had been cowed by British war preparations. The long-term threat to the Northern cause continued, however, as Britain and France stepped up their campaign to lift the blockade of cotton imports and to resolve the threat to international commerce by U.S. naval forces. Charles Francis Adams and Thomas Dudley were now required to turn all their attention to the Confederate program to create a modern navy of steam-powered warships in British shipyards.

CHAPTER 3

A Nest of Pirates

When the U.S. Civil War broke out, both North and South expected a short war, and neither side possessed the material and manpower required for what would prove to be the first modern industrialized war. Both were soon forced to adapt to the requirements of a protracted conflict by the total mobilization of the resources available to each. The North, however, held a distinct advantage in naval forces. James McPherson notes that by the end of 1861, at the time when Thomas Dudley took over the consulate in Liverpool, the Union had more than 260 warships on active duty blockading the coasts and river towns of the South and were constructing 100 more.

The Confederate states, on the other hand, had "no navy and few facilities for building one. The South possessed no adequate shipyards except the captured naval yard at Norfolk, and not a single machine shop capable of building an engine large enough to power a respectable warship." But while the South lacked material resources for a proper navy, McPherson argues that it possessed "striking human resources," namely Secretary of the Confederate Navy Stephen Mallory and Commanders James Bulloch and Raphael Semmes.[1] These three capable men were dedicated to breaking the Northern blockade, providing foreign arms for Southern armies, and building large steam-powered warships in British shipyards. The major obstacle to their success would prove to be Lincoln's consul in Liverpool, Thomas Haines Dudley.

James Bulloch arrived in Liverpool on June 4, 1861, some six months before Dudley put in his appearance at the port. Bulloch reports in his memoirs that within a month of his arrival at Liverpool, he had begun the purchase

27

of large quantities of naval supplies on credit and had laid the keel of the first foreign-built Confederate cruiser.

The State Department was aware of Confederate secret activities in Britain from the beginning of the war, and Secretary Seward lost no time in establishing the North's intelligence system to counter Confederate operations in Europe. Coordination of this network, designed for gathering information on Confederate shipbuilding and the purchase of munitions and military supplies, was placed under the direction of Henry Shelton Sanford, who had been appointed minister to Belgium in March 1861. The other key member of the Union's European intelligence organization in Europe was Freeman Harlow Morse, the U.S. consul in London.

The two coordinators of intelligence soon found themselves in conflict over the goals and operational procedures of the U.S. intelligence mission against Confederate agents in their main base of operations in Britain. Morse believed that any surveillance by the Union network of Rebel operations should not jeopardize Anglo-American diplomatic relations, while Sanford was convinced that covert activity should be directed at preventing the shipment of Rebel war materials from British ports. Sanford, who turned out to be one of the many rogue operators to plague American spy agencies over the centuries, lost no time in planning direct sabotage of Confederate ships and war supplies in England. The two men reflected the classic conflict produced by all intelligence operations: whether covert action is intended to supplement the aims of the State Department or the War Department.[2]

Henry Sanford had considerable experience in the diplomatic service of the United States. He had served as an attaché in St. Petersburg in 1847, was acting secretary of the legation at Frankfurt from 1849 to 1854, had served as chargé d'affaires in Paris, and possessed a broad range of influential contacts in Europe. Freeman Harlow Morse, on the other hand, had, like Thomas Dudley, been appointed to his consular post by Lincoln for political reasons. Morse had served in Congress for a number of years and been head of the Republican organization in Maine. His application for consular service was supported by leading shipowners in New York City and most members of Congress. He took up his consular duties on May 25 and established an office on Grace Church Street in London, within walking distance of the home of Charles Francis Adams.

In the six months preceding Dudley's arrival in Liverpool, Sanford and Morse had organized a network of detectives to spy on Rebel activities. Their reports were delivered directly to both Sanford and Morse. On July 4, 1861, Sanford wrote to Seward of his plan to "get at the operations" of Rebel agents by hiring local spies. "How it will be done, whether through a pretty mistress or a spying landlord is nobody's business; but I lay stress on getting you full accounts of their operations here. I go on the doctrine that in war as in love everything is fair that will lead to success."[3]

Henry Wilding, the acting consul in Liverpool before Dudley's appointment, was an active participant in the Sanford-Morse network. The State Department was aware of the appointment of James Dunwoody Bulloch as the head of the Confederate Secret Service in England and warned Wilding to keep a lookout for the Confederate agent's arrival in Britain. Wilding wrote to Charles Francis Adams on July 3, saying that the State Department had informed him of Bulloch's departure for England, but that he had "not been able to get any trace of him in Liverpool, beyond a vague statement that a person answering his description was here about two weeks since and has gone to Glasgow." Wilding added, "I shall continue my inquiries and let you know the results as early as possible."[4]

Finally, on September 12, Wilding tracked down the leading Confederate agent in Britain. Wilding reported to Adams, "Captain J. D. Bulloch referred to in your letter of the 20 July is here in private lodgings." Shortly afterward, Wilding informed him: "Captain Bulloch left here for London by the mail train last evening. While here has been chiefly in communication with Fraser-Trenholm & Co., and no doubt has something to do with the two steamers bought by them. He is a very dark, sallow man with black hair and eyes, whiskers down each cheek but shaved clean off his chin and below, dark moustache, about 5'8" high. He went alone and took little luggage."[5] Another communication from Wilding informed the London center: "There came also in the *Edinberg* a female named Leone Sarvan said to be a bearer of despatches from Richmond. She is a native of New Orleans, about 30, good looking. She left this morning for London by the 10:30 train."[6] The U.S. spy network was off to a good start.

In the summer of 1861, Sanford was sending reports to the State Department concerning a Rebel ship that Bulloch had had loaded with munitions and armaments. The ship was the *Bermuda*, English owned and outfitted by the Liverpool firm of Fraser, Trenholm and Company. Sanford's information again came from Henry Wilding, the capable acting consul in Liverpool, who was soon to become Dudley's key aide. Sanford requested that a Union warship be put in position to intercept the *Bermuda* once it put out to sea.

By the end of September, Sanford proposed that he head an enlarged network of spies in England. "The question must immediately be decided: are we strong enough to permit the enemy to be supplied with means for carrying on the war? If not, we must spend money here."[7]

Sanford left little doubt that his intention was to replace Morse as the head of intelligence in England, the main base of Confederate operations. In his correspondence to Seward, Sanford was openly critical of Morse for having allowed a ship to leave England with seventy tons of Rebel contraband and argued that Morse should have devised a plan to sabotage it. "5000 pounds would have sunk her, accidents are so numerous in the Channel you know!"[8] Seward replied that the Union blockade, and not sabotage, would stop munitions shipments to the South. In fact, the ship Sanford had accused Morse of allowing to escape was captured by U.S. warships when it attempted to run the blockade into a Southern port, and the State Department thanked Morse for his prompt information leading to the capture of the steamer *Thomas Watson*.

Sanford, like many other prominent operators in the history of U.S. intelligence, had a penchant for covert action. Morse complained to Sanford that J. Pollacky, the chief detective working for Sanford in London, was overpaid and seemed to be of "no great advantage." He added, "His men are bold and open in dogging people which creates no little talk." Morse wanted Pollacky discharged. At the same time, Charles Francis Adams, who was determined not to have his own position compromised by association with intelligence operations, told Morse that members of Parliament sympathetic to the North had informed the American minister that open and brazen provocative actions by Northern agents were injuring the Union cause and contributing to adverse English public opinion. Morse subsequently wrote Sanford that he was discharging the London detective and that he would have nothing further to do with him. Sanford, however, went on to hatch even more adventurous schemes.[9]

On October 29, Sanford wrote Seward that he had learned from his agents that a Rebel contraband ship would soon leave from a North Sea port, and that he had employed a U.S. merchant marine captain, Edwin Eastman, to sign on the ship and bribe the crew to sail the vessel into a Union port. A week later, Sanford wrote Seward that Eastman was unable to get a berth on the ship but planned to bribe the pilot of the *Gladiator*, a seven-hundred-ton ship bought by the Confederates and preparing to leave London with a full cargo, to run the ship aground on a mud bank in the River Thames on November 6. Sanford's scheme called for a U.S. warship, the *James Adgar*, cruising in English waters, to enter the Thames and seize the Confederate ship. According to Neil Sanders's research, Sanford informed Charles Francis Adams of this operation but was not completely candid with the minister. Adams agreed that he would cooperate with Eastman if the plans for the U.S. warship were outside the jurisdiction of any neutral power. Neil Sanders concludes, "It is impossible to believe that Sanford informed Adams that his scheme involved a mud-bank in the Thames."[10]

Fortunately, Sanford's various plots and scenarios fell through. The scheme to ground and then seize the Confederate ship *Gladiator* in the Thames, occurring as it did during the very month of the *Trent* incident, might well have tipped the balance for war in the English cabinet. Seward and the State Department had decided to put a muzzle on Sanford even before they'd learned of his latest provocative brainstorm. Sanford was dismissed as chief of intelligence in Europe because he threatened to violate English neutrality. On November 4, two weeks before Dudley arrived in Liverpool, the assistant secretary of state sent a dispatch to Sanford in Brussels informing him:

> The Department appreciates your active and intelligent services in detecting traitorous proceedings against this government in England. Some inconveniences have, however, resulted from the fact that the regular agents of this government in that country have also been authorized to perform services of that character. Consequently, as in the future it is deemed best to entrust Mr. Morse, the United States Consul at London, with the sole charge of that business in that country, you will direct the persons in your employment there to report to him and be governed by him.[11]

Sanford remained as minister to Belgium but was removed from all connections with the sensitive intelligence operations in England. Seward and the State Department created an entirely new intelligence-gathering system for England, to be coordinated by Morse in London and Dudley in Liverpool. Its mission was to combine intelligence against Confederate operations in England with the diplomatic effort to guarantee English neutrality, prevent British recognition of the South, and make use of the British legal system to close down the Confederate shipbuilding program in England. In addition, U.S. intelligence operations would continue to provide the U.S. Navy with information on all Rebel blockade-running operations.

Although the London consul continued to play a major role in the intelligence network, Dudley soon supplanted Morse as the major U.S. operative in Britain. Within a few months, because of his energy, ability, and dogged determination, and because he was operating in the major base of Confederate activities, Thomas Haines Dudley would take over as the *de facto* U.S. intelligence director in England. He was soon placed in a position to oversee and direct all the consulates in the British Isles, except London, where Morse retained his authority. The system of consuls became the framework for Union intelligence operations in Britain. Minister Charles Francis Adams stayed aloof from all of these operations in order to devote himself to diplomacy, but without the information Dudley provided him, his diplomatic mission would have been fruitless.

During his first months in Liverpool, Thomas Dudley energetically built up and improved the intelligence apparatus he had inherited from Sanford and Morse. Dudley and Wilding made a good team. Wilding had employed a very capable British private detective, Matthew Maguire, whom Dudley retained and gave three assistants to spy on covert Confederate operations. Dudley lost no time in constructing a network of Northern sympathizers and British shipyard workers to expand his information on Southern secret activities. At the same time, he energetically pursued his role of open diplomacy and shouldered the burdens of routine consular affairs.

Dudley's work was often unpleasant and dangerous. From the time of his arrival, he was subjected to insults and threats from Confederate agents and sympathizers. Enemies of the North tied tin kettles and bricks to the flag flying from the U.S. consular offices. On one occasion, three burly men, apparently armed, attempted to force their way through the front door of the consulate past Dudley's terrified housekeeper. The consul himself stepped into the doorway, thrust the men back, slammed the door, and bolted it against the presumed assassins.[12]

Dudley had not been long in Liverpool before he received letters telling him that if he were found near specific shipyards and dock areas of the port, he would be shot on the spot. None of these threats deterred Consul Dudley, who often toured the dock area, where he could be found with his binoculars surveying the scene of Confederate activity. There is no record of whether Dudley went out armed, but it would be surprising if he did not. During his years of travel from Liverpool to London and the northern dock areas of Scotland, he often traveled incognito and was careful to throw off trailing Confederate agents. Dudley quickly mastered the techniques required of a public representative of the United States, while at the same time managing a widespread covert spy network.

As a practicing Quaker and experienced lawyer, Thomas Dudley did not enjoy the deceptions necessary for a successful espionage operation. The new consul reported to Seward on December 12 on the difficulty of enlisting spies against the Confederates. Although he wanted only trustworthy men, Dudley noted that the ones he found were "not as a general thing very esteemable men, but are the only persons we can get to engage in this business, which I am sure you will agree with me is not a very pleasant one. They require to be well paid. Their service will cost two thousand dollars to make it efficient."[13]

Dudley's papers and the archives of the State Department reveal the unceasing flow of information he gathered and forwarded to Seward and Adams on ship sailings, blockade runners, descriptions of munitions purchased by the Confederacy, and other activities of Rebel agents in Great Britain. Dudley's espionage apparatus was aided by shipyard workers and other British citizens sympathetic to the Northern cause.

An example of such aid is revealed in a letter to Dudley dated December 2, 1862, from a Robert Walker and posted from Birkenhead. The letter informed Dudley of the departure of the steam packet *Douglas,* identified as a blockade runner so deeply loaded with coal that her decks were within eighteen inches of the water. The informant clearly expressed his support for the antislavery cause:

> She is bound for Nassau and is intended to run the blockade with contraband of war to the rebels and slaveholders, but whether she goes direct to sea this day or not I cannot say. There is no doubt you will get all particulars to that and I hope such means will be adopted as will give the Federal Government vessels of war a chance to capture her when breaking the law of nations (International Law) and thereby aiding Rebellion. My sympathy for the free institutions of the Great Republic and the Slave Emancipation Proclamation of President Lincoln and my hatred of slave institutions and the willful law breaking and lying assertions of secession sympathizers in Great Britain and Ireland.[14]

An informant, code-named Federal, sent Dudley lists of Confederate agents in Britain. Other sources turned over an intercepted letter from James Bulloch to Stephen Russell Mallory, secretary of the Confederate navy, reporting on a reconnaissance of the Cape Fear River and assessing the chances of Confederate ships breaking out of the blockade.

On March 22, Federal wrote to Dudley:

> Captain John Law who went out in the Fingal returned to Liverpool in the Annie Childs. He has again left the Mersey this morning for the Confederate States in a new screw steamer built by Miller with a very heavy and valuable cargo, it is supposed from her trial trip there is nothing in the American waters can catch her. She is now the

property and has been freighted by Captain Low's two relatives W. Low and W. Green who are now prisoners on parole in the United States, the money has been found by the office of Green and Low and Co., Liverpool. Bets have been made that Captain Low will return in less than three months time laden with cotton.[15]

In addition to managing his own agents, Dudley coordinated the information provided by the consuls throughout the British Isles. John Young from Belfast, referring to the ship *Adela,* docked in Liverpool, informed Dudley in May that the ship would shortly start to run the blockade and that her captain was named Walker. "You will do well to have some sharp man to play the game on the captain and find out her destination," he advised. "Then report the matter instantly to Seward." John Prettyman in Glasgow supplemented the information received from Belfast, informing Dudley that the steamer *Adela* "has been purchased here by a Liverpool house and ordered to Liverpool. It is suspected to be fitted out for service of the American rebels."[16] Dudley's network rapidly achieved remarkable efficiency. Southern agents in Britain were well aware of the effectiveness of the counterespionage operation directed against them by the Liverpool consul.

Thomas Dudley's most formidable adversary proved to be James Bulloch, who had been sent to Britain by the Confederacy together with James North to purchase arms and construct a Confederate navy. In the early months of 1862, Dudley and Wilding uncovered Bulloch's secret shipbuilding program. This Southern naval program was financed by the prestigious Liverpool firm of Fraser, Trenholm and Company, which bankrolled the purchase of armaments by the South throughout the Civil War.

By February 3, Dudley was reporting to the State Department on a "screw gunboat called the *Oreto*" being built in a Liverpool shipyard:

> The builders say she is intended for the Italian Government. Fawcett Preston & Co. are fitting her out, supplying all the machinery etc. From this fact and some other suspicious circumstances I am afraid she is intended for the South. She has one funnel, three masts, bark rigged, eight port holes on each side and is to carry sixteen guns. Her coal is now being put on board and she will go to sea most likely the latter part of the week. Her armament is not as yet on board and the appearances indicate that she is to leave Liverpool and receive (armaments) at some other place.[17]

Dudley checked with the Italian consul, who told him that he had "no knowledge of this vessel being built or intended for the Italian Government."

Wilding wrote a note to Dudley in March informing him that Minister Adams "is greatly pleased" with the information provided on the *Oreto.*

Dudley's network had uncovered the first of the great Confederate cruisers to be commissioned in England. The *Oreto* was to become the infamous *Florida,* which would ravage Northern merchant shipping in the months ahead. Dudley and Adams immediately launched a long diplomatic and legal fight to prevent the escape of the *Florida* and subsequently the even more formidable *Alabama,* which Dudley and Wilding were soon to discover.

On February 15, Dudley reported on an immense quantity of arms and munitions being shipped from Liverpool to the west coast of Africa, "much more than any legitimate trade with that coast would seem to warrant." He speculated that these shipments would be reloaded onto Southern blockade runners at Madeira or one of the other western islands. Two days later, Dudley was again reporting on the *Oreto.* "She is to make a trial trip in the river today. No armaments as yet on board. She has put up a second smoke stack since I last wrote you."[18]

By the middle of March, Dudley informed Charles Francis Adams that the Oreto had returned and was "apparently waiting for someone." That someone was "Captain Bullock [*sic*] the man who went out in the Bermuda on her first passage" and returned "as a passenger on the steamer Annie Childs which ran the blockade at Wilmington, N.C. about the middle of last month and arrived at the port yesterday with 700 bales of cotton consigned to Fraser Trenholm."[19] By the third week in March, Dudley was reporting to Seward describing the *Oreto* with "Bullock" as the commander. James Bulloch would never again operate in secrecy in the British Isles.

James Dunwoody Bulloch, a former U.S. Navy officer who had spent fourteen years in the navy and eight years in commercial shipping, possessed the rare expertise necessary for overseeing the construction of Confederate warships in Britain. Entrusted with vast sums of money by Stephen Mallory, secretary of the Confederate navy, Bulloch combined the skill, social graces, and business acumen to make him the most formidable Southern secret agent in Europe. In the fall of 1861, Bulloch purchased a recently built fast steamer, loaded it with Enfield rifles and large stocks of munitions, took command of the ship himself, and in a daring voyage, ran it through the blockade into Savannah. He then returned to England, where he continued his secret activities to build warships for the South. One historian marks Bulloch's contribution to the Confederacy as second only to that of Robert E. Lee.

In his memoirs, Bulloch comments on his adversary Dudley as being "grieved and vexed" at the Confederate ability to circumvent the British Foreign Enlistment Act and notes that Dudley's "suspicions having been once aroused, his mind was kept in a wakeful and agitated condition during the remainder of the war." Once the Confederate shipbuilding program was under way in Liverpool shipyards, Bulloch complained, "I soon learned that spies were lurking about, and tampering with the workmen at Messrs. Laird's, and that a private detective named Maguire was taking a deep and abiding interest in my personal movements."[20] The duel between Dudley, the North's master spy, and Bulloch, head of the Confederate Secret Service in Europe, opened up a new crucial front in the American Civil War.

CHAPTER 4

The Escape of the
Confederate Cruisers

WHILE BULLOCH WAS HARASSED BY SPIES, DUDLEY CONFRONTED A LIVERPOOL establishment of shippers, manufacturers, merchants, city newspapers, and government officials who supported the Confederacy. Dudley, as a lawyer, was determined to utilize the Foreign Enlistment Act of 1819 to prevent the building of Confederate ships in British yards. This act forbade anyone within the British Empire to "equip, furnish, fit out, or arm" a ship with the intent that such vessel be used for military purposes against a nation "with which his Majesty shall not then be at war."

Minister Adams turned over the evidence Dudley had collected on the *Oreto* to the Foreign Office in the middle of March. As a result, the Foreign Office gave instructions to the customs officials at Liverpool to investigate the ship. Since the vessel was not armed, the customs officers, by a very technical reading of the Foreign Enlistment Act, determined that it was not a warship and that there was no cause to detain it. Dudley had come up against Samuel Price Edwards, Her Majesty's collector of customs at Liverpool, whom history would record as, at most, a paid agent of the Confederacy and, at the least, an ardent Confederate sympathizer.[1] Dudley and Adams were naturally infuriated by the decision. The American minister was ready to make another appeal to Russell, but the foreign secretary had left London. In the meantime, Bulloch sailed the gunboat out of Liverpool on March 22 and put her under the command of a British captain. The first Confederate cruiser built in British shipyards had escaped.

James Dunwoody Bulloch and Thomas Haines Dudley were soon engaged in a classic contest of intelligence and counterintelligence operations.

Bulloch was an able organizer and administrator who showed great skill in manipulating the narrow construction of the Foreign Enlistment Act. In addition, his task was made easier by Confederate sympathizers in official positions throughout England. Bulloch's memoirs reveal the stratagems, ruses, and disguises employed in the escape of the *Florida* and *Alabama,* but they also reveal that Bulloch was able to keep very little secret from the intelligence operation Thomas Dudley mounted against him. Bulloch's strategy, as Dudley soon found out, was to build his steam gunboats under the guise that they were ordinary steamers, and then to arm them either at sea or in the Azores or West Indies. In the case of the *Oreto* or *Florida,* Bulloch records that he had "made a thorough investigation, and satisfied myself that not a single article contraband of war was on board the ship—not a weapon, not an appliance for mounting a gun. In this condition I was advised that according to the Municipal Law of Great Britain, she was a perfectly lawful article of traffic, the builder could deliver her, and I could pay for and receive her, without infringing any statute, or transgressing any requirement of commercial propriety."[2]

The Confederate captain's claim of legality was, in fact, undermined by the many subterfuges employed to get his raiders out of England, all of which were uncovered and documented by Dudley and Wilder. First was to disguise the true owner of the ship; second, to employ a certified British captain to take the ship out; and third, to conceal the true destination of the voyage. In the case of the *Florida,* the crew signed on for a voyage from Liverpool to Palermo because the ship was supposed to be under Italian ownership, but instead, the ship went directly to the West Indies, where it would receive its armament. Bulloch's letter to Capt. John Maffitt, who was to command the *Florida,* to be forwarded to the Confederate secretary of the navy, Mallory, clearly reveals his strategy for building a Confederate navy in British yards:

> Liverpool, 21st March, 1862
>
> Sir,
>
> Day after tomorrow I despatch for Nassau a gun-vessel, built in England under contract with me for the Confederate Navy. In all sailing and steaming equipment she is very complete, but I have been forced to dispense with all outfit suited to her true character. It has been with much difficulty, and only by the most cautious management, that she has escaped seizure or indefinite detention here, and I send her as she is, the first regularly built war-vessel for our Navy, to your care. . . .
>
> It has been impossible to get the regular battery intended for her on board, but I have sent out four 7-inch rifled guns, with all neces-

sary equipments in the steamship Bahama, bound to Nassau, and Mr. Low will give you all particulars as to her probable time of arrival, and will also hand you a list of every-thing on board the gun-vessel, as well as an invoice of the shipment by the Bahama. Another ship will be ready in about two months, and I will take the sea in her myself by some means or other, although I perceive many difficulties looming in the future.[3]

When Lord Russell returned to London, he appeared ready to execute an order for the seizure of the *Oreto*, but she was already on the high seas en route to Nassau. The *Oreto* sailed to the West Indies, where she was armed and commissioned into the Confederate navy as the *Florida*, later to become the scourge of Northern merchant shipping. In June, Union representatives in the West Indies presented evidence to British authorities for the detention of the *Florida* for violation of the Foreign Enlistment Act. A vice admiralty court, however, released the *Florida* on the grounds that it could not prove the warship had been equipped for war in English territory.[4] Dudley and Adams again were incensed with this decision, because it indicated that the English had little intention of preventing the construction and operation of Rebel warships. Dudley, however, was determined to use the British legal system and diplomatic pressure as weapons to outlaw the construction and launching of Confederate warships and get the British to enforce their own laws.

After weeks of surveillance, Dudley, Wilding, and their secret agents discovered a second Confederate cruiser under construction in Liverpool. Dudley reported to the State Department on April 4 that this gunboat of eleven hundred tons was the exact model of the *Florida*, with engines of three hundred horsepower. The ship was being built in the Birkenhead Ironworks, a yard owned by John Laird and his sons. The firm had been building iron ships since 1829 and had an international reputation for building first-class vessels. Laird later turned the business over to his sons, entered Parliament, and became a forceful British advocate for the Confederacy.

Dudley immediately wrote to Adams to report that one of the Laird brothers had told a British Army officer that the ship was for the Spanish government. Dudley wanted Adams to make an inquiry at the Spanish embassy concerning the vessel. Adams was soon given assurance that the warship, called the 290 in the shipyard, was not being built for Spain.[5] Consul Dudley then began to provide a day-to-day report on all the activities surrounding the 290.

Dudley's operation discovered that two officers from the Confederate warship *Sumter*, Lieutenant Beauford and Gunner Caddy, had passed through Liverpool and stated that a Southern cruiser was under construction in the

Lairds' yard. The report was confirmed by a leading workman in the shipyard, who told Dudley that the 290 was being built for the South. By the middle of May, Dudley was able to give a full report to Secretary of State Seward on the configuration and details of the ship:

> She will be when finished a very superior boat, her planks were caulked as they were put on, her timbers are of the very best English oak, every plank & timber was most critically examined, and all her fastenings are copper bolts 18 feet long 2 ½ & 3 ½ inches in circumference. The steam gear is all copper and brass, in a word the foreman who had charge of building her says that no boat was ever built stronger or better than her. The order when given was to build her of the very best material and in the best & strongest manner without regard to expence and the foreman says this has been done. . . . There is no doubt but what she is intended for the Rebels.[6]

The Confederate warship was soon launched, and in the middle of June, Dudley's agents reported that she was making a trial run up the Mersey River. In the meantime, Wilding was working full-time to penetrate the mysteries of the 290. On July 3, he reported that "W. A. Blain of 35 Paradise Street was employed to fit up the cabins. His foreman stated that Mr. Laird paid for the fittings & furniture, but they were selected & approved by Captain Bulloch."[7]

Two days later, Wilding revealed that Bulloch had gone into the private dock of the 290, boarded the ship, and "was greeted by the workmen and gave orders as a person in charge." Wilding also furnished a statement by the *Julia*'s second mate, who had been in the Rebel army and wished to ship on a blockade runner being loaded in Liverpool. He "brags that he will get to New Orleans and will shoot General Butler if he is hung for it the next day. I haven't his name but it shall be got and sent to you." Both Wilding and Maguire frequented Liverpool taverns and were rewarded for their efforts.

In the month of July, Dudley's ring had penetrated deep into the lair of the 290. The consul took a few days off to visit his friend Dayton, U.S. minister to Paris, and while there, his health problems plagued him once again. On July 4, Dudley wrote to Wilding, "I am quite ill today and can scarcely muster strength to write this note." But sickness rarely interfered with Dudley's Quaker devotion to duty. He went on to say that he had received two letters Wilding had written on July 1 and 2. Wilding had wished to issue a license from the consulate authorizing passage for a ship delivering coal to a Mexican port. Dudley objected because he believed the coal was destined for the South and thought that this would be as much a violation of the blockade as if the ship were destined for New Orleans. Dudley concluded, "I do not see as I understand the case that we ought to license her. I shall be home by Thursday next if I do not get better by Tuesday."[8]

A week later, Dudley sent off a dispatch to the secretary of state informing him that Richard Braugan, a shipwright in the employ of the Lairds, had told him that on the day the 290 was launched, Captain Bulloch, his wife, and a number of gentlemen were present. Bulloch was on the scene every day and gave orders to the shipbuilders as an owner of the vessel. Braugan reported that Bulloch openly presented himself as a representative of the Southern states, and that there was no question that the ship was a privateer in the same class as the *Oreto*.

The plan was for the 290 and the *Oreto* to cruise together on the American coast as Confederate raiders. A man by the name of Matthew Butcher was to go out as the nominal captain of the warship and was presently recruiting a crew. Braugan was asked to ship as a carpenter, and a man named Barnet was filling the role of acting shipping master. The next day, Dudley sent Seward the exact dimensions of the new Confederate cruiser, including the length of the keel, its depth, breadth, and other details.

During his fruitless efforts to prevent the escape of the 290, Dudley's pessimism concerning British public opinion increased. He wrote to Seward that the "reverse of McClellan before Richmond has caused the feeling in this country against the United States and in favor of the South to break out afresh and with increasing virulence. Men who advocated the South in secret now do it openly. Those who pretended to be neutral now show themselves in their favor and the few who have been with us here become neutral or silenced by the clamor. The current is against us and it is strong and threatens to carry everything with it."[9]

Dudley went on to express his fear that the "danger of intervention" was more serious than it had ever been and stated, "I am fully persuaded that if we are not successful in some decisive battle within a short period this government will be forced to acknowledge the Confederacy or else be driven from office." The consul then suggested that nothing could enforce neutrality among European nations more effectively than a large increase in the commission of ironclad ships for the Federal navy. "If I was in Congress knowing what I do of the sentiments of Europe I should urge with all my power and ability the immediate construction of at least 30 additional Monitors." He argued that the building of ironclad ships would do more than diplomacy to prevent intervention in the war by Britain and France. "It is fear not love that will prevent interference."

A few months earlier, Dudley had written Seward:

[I had] hoped that the fall of New Orleans, the evacuation of York-town, and our other successes at home with the prospect of a speedy termination of the rebellion would have the effect to discourage the friends and allies of the Rebels in this country & prevent the fitting out of other vessels and expeditions to aid them in the unholy work of trying to destroy the government. But contrary to my hopes and expectations it seems not to have any effect on them. The business goes on as lively and actively as at any previous period.[10]

Despite his ill health and depressed state of mind, Dudley doggedly per-sisted in his campaign to uncover Confederate covert operations in Britain. In early June, he forwarded to Washington a long list of British firms supplying the South and fitting out ships to run the Northern blockade of Southern ports. Even more important was the success of Dudley's ring in penetrating Bulloch's secret construction of Confederate warships.

Secretary of State Seward was pleased with the flow of information the Liverpool consul was providing. He wrote to Dudley on June 4: "The Depart-ment is gratified to be able to inform you, that several of the steamers . . . conveying stores and contraband to the rebels, and of which you gave the Department early and exact information, have been captured in the attempt to run the blockade; the information which you communicated having been conveyed by the Secretary of the Navy to the officers of the blockading squadron."[11]

Some time later, Seward informed Dudley that the *Princess Royal,* a vessel Dudley had alerted Federal authorities to be a blockade runner, had been cap-tured. Seward wrote: "The Navy Department, in this case, as in many others, was seasonably apprised of her intention to elude the blockade through the information communicated by yourself . . . and was thus enabled to prevent the supplies with which she was loaded from going into the possession of the rebels."[12]

Dudley's chief detective, Matthew Maguire, who spent a good deal of his time in waterfront taverns, one day befriended a young Southern seaman named Robinson, who had landed in Liverpool after making a cruise on the blockade runner *Julia Usher.* Dudley's detective even persuaded the young sailor to take lodging at his house. Robinson, having no idea who Maguire was, confided to him that he had heard the captain and officers of his ship describe a gunboat being built by the Lairds for the Confederate navy. The young sailor told Maguire that Bulloch would command her, and that she would sail as a raider without ever having to run the blockade or put into a

Southern port. Moreover, the young man reported that Fraser, Trenholm and Company was financing the construction of the warship.

Wilding wrote a note to Dudley on June 19, informing him that Robinson had told Maguire that the new Confederate gunboat would not make any attempt to run the blockade, but was planned to operate as a privateer mounting eleven guns. "The boy is very anxious to join the gunboat himself and wants Maguire to speak to Captain Bulloch for him. He makes these statements to Maguire in entire ignorance that Maguire has any connection with us."[13] Dudley's spy ring could hardly be asked for more accurate intelligence than this.

Dudley went up to London to see Adams and, while there, presented the minister with all his evidence collected on the Confederate cruiser and told him that he planned to make a formal application to the collector of customs in Liverpool, demanding British seizure of the ship under the Foreign Enlistment Act. Adams believed the better course would be to submit Dudley's evidence directly to the Foreign Office.

The minister therefore submitted Dudley's evidence to Lord Russell on June 23 with a request that such action be taken "as may tend either to stop the projected expedition, or to establish the fact that its purpose is not inimical to the people of the United States." Russell, in turn, forwarded the information on the 290 to the law officers of the Crown. The law officers quickly determined that if Dudley's facts were accurate, the construction of the 290 was a manifest violation of the Foreign Enlistment Act and steps should be taken to prevent the ship from sailing. The lords commissioners of the Treasury who supervised the Customs Department came up with a different opinion. They forwarded to Russell the finding of the customs collector at Liverpool that the ship was undoubtedly a warship, but that there were not sufficient grounds to warrant its detention. They suggested that Dudley submit his evidence to the Board of Customs.[14]

Dudley and Adams now had to face the bureaucratic runaround that would become the standard procedure in their dealings with the British Foreign Office. Even worse, it was now clear that Lord Russell and the British authorities would put the total burden of proof on the Liverpool consul to substantiate his charges. Dudley suspected that Price Edwards, the Liverpool collector, was a Confederate agent, and the consul was extremely reluctant to reveal his sources to such a man.

Dudley faced the dilemma often confronting intelligence officers. Much of his information came from friends of the North or from paid informers. How could he substantiate his evidence with signed affidavits and at the same time protect his sources? Dudley attempted to resolve the dilemma by submitting a lengthy and detailed statement to the customs collector specifying all the evidence he had collected to confirm that the 290 was a Confederate warship. The collector admitted that the 290 might be a Confederate cruiser, but the charges Dudley and Wilding had submitted did not, in his opinion, meet the legal requirement of evidence supported by signed affidavits from firsthand witnesses.

The collector agreed, however, to send Dudley's statement of evidence to the Board of Customs for review. While anxiously awaiting a reply, Dudley and Wilding observed the departure of the 290 from the Lairds' yard out into the Great Float at Birkenhead. There the ship took on supplies and five hundred tons of coal. The Board of Customs, after weighing Dudley's evidence, replied that "there does not appear to be prima facie proof sufficient in the statement of the consul to justify the seizure of the vessel."[15]

Charles Francis Adams, perhaps not sufficiently aware of the problem Dudley faced in the attempt to protect his intelligence agents, criticized him for being remiss by not supporting his statement with legal affidavits and requested that he do so. Dudley replied that if he carried out the minister's request, he would be put in an embarrassing position. "The persons whom I have in my employ do not want me to give their names." By exposing his informants, Dudley argued, their usefulness to him in the future would be destroyed.

Nevertheless, Adams sent a copy of Dudley's letter of July 9 to the queen's counsel, member of Parliament and judge advocate of the Admiralty, Robert Collier. One week later, Collier gave a definitive reply: "I think the evidence almost conclusive that the vessel in question is being fitted out by the Messrs. Laird as a privateer for the use of the Confederate government, in contravention of the provisions of the foreign enlistment act." Collier concluded that "it would be proper . . . to lay a statement of the fact before the secretary of state for foreign affairs, coupled with a request that Her Majesty's government would direct the vessel to be seized, or ratify her seizure if it had been made."[16]

Adams, naturally delighted with this response, asked Dudley to follow Collier's advice and employ a trusted solicitor to draw up the papers in acceptable British legal form. Dudley hired the English lawyer A. F. Squarey, and though Dudley was still worried about procuring direct signed evidence, Squarey believed they could collect enough evidence to stop the South's new cruiser. Dudley and Squarey then worked night and day to draw up six separate affidavits detailing the evidence that the 290 was a Confederate warship.

The evidence was massive. The first two affidavits put together by Dudley and the detective Maguire linked Bulloch definitively with the Confederacy and the 290, another by a public clerk identified the ship in question as the 290, another put together by a local shipping master established Bulloch's connection with the *Oreto*, now the *Florida*, under seizure by the local authorities in Nassau. A fifth deposition, put together by Wilding and Maguire, spelled out the evidence provided by Richard Brogan, the Lairds' young shipwright. A sixth affidavit supplied new direct and firsthand evidence. It was a deposition by a sailor and man-of-war's man, William Passmore. He stated that he had been enlisted by Captain Butcher, the English captain hired by Bulloch, and that Butcher had told him that the 290 was to become a Confederate cruiser and would fight for the South. Passmore reported that thirty seamen, most of whom had had experience on warships, had been recruited to man the 290. In addition, he stated that Captain Bulloch was aboard the ship every day and would command the 290 once it put to sea.[17]

Dudley and Squarey went up to London to present these affidavits to Charles Adams, who then immediately forwarded copies to the Foreign Office. Dudley's agents in Liverpool continued to collect evidence and soon came up with two more affidavits from seamen who were to sail on the 290. These firsthand witnesses supported the evidence affirmed by Passmore that the vessel was a war vessel destined for the Confederacy and that Bulloch was to be her commander. Subsequently, a ninth affidavit was put together by another seaman aboard the 290, confirming all the statements made by the first three.

While the 290 made open preparations for its escape, Dudley and Adams continued their frantic legal struggle to stop her. What they faced was the legal labyrinth of English law satirized so brilliantly in the novels of Charles Dickens. Dudley and Squarey went directly to the Board of Customs in London to present their affidavits and were told that the collector in Liverpool had already rejected their application for seizure based on the first six affidavits. They then returned to Collier, the queen's counsel, with all their new evidence, and he responded with a second definitive opinion: "It appears difficult to make out a stronger case of infringement of the foreign enlistment act, which, if not enforced on this occasion, is little better than a dead letter." He added that if the ship were allowed to sail, the U.S. government would have "serious grounds for remonstrance."[18] The papers were then passed back and forth among the Customs Board, the Foreign Office, the law officers, and the lords of the Treasury. Lord Russell finally ordered that the law officers, the highest legal officials in the government, review the case.

Dudley, no doubt weary of what was becoming a comic opera, returned to Liverpool, hired a photographer to take pictures of the gunboat, and began negotiations with a sailor whom he wished to employ as a spy on the ship. Dudley soon learned that the crew of the 290 had been ordered to report on board on July 28. It was obvious that the ship was about to sail. On the twenty-ninth, with flags flying and a host of Confederate celebrants aboard, the future *Alabama,* ostensibly on a trial run, but in fact never to return, steamed up the Mersey River on her way to the open ocean. The legal charade played on to its Dickensian conclusion.

While Bulloch was preparing for the escape of the 290, Dudley's documents had been forwarded to the queen's advocate, Sir John Harding, who was responsible for passing them on to the attorney general and the solicitor general. The problem, however, was that John Harding had suffered a mental breakdown, had in fact resigned from office, and had been sent to stay with friends in Reading. It was not until July 28 that the legal advisors who had been waiting for a reply found out that Harding had been declared legally insane and had carried off Dudley's documents to the asylum, refusing to give them up.

When the documents were finally retrieved, they were sent to Attorney General Atherton. The law officers quickly upheld Collier's broad interpretation of the Foreign Enlistment Act. Their interpretation went beyond the narrow construction of the clause "to equip, furnish, fit out or arm" on the basis that it "would fritter away the Act, and give impunity to open and flagrant violations of its provisions." They recommended immediate seizure of the 290, but Lord Russell was again out of town, and Bulloch used every minute of British delay to plot the ship's escape.[19]

Bulloch complains in his memoirs of the "irritating persistency" of the U.S. consul in Liverpool in attempting to get British authorities to seize or detain the 290 while it lay in the Lairds' shipyard. The warship was launched on May 15, and Bulloch asserts that "no mystery or disguise was attempted" to conceal the purpose of the ship, since he was careful to observe the narrow interpretation of the Foreign Enlistment Act that it was not technically a warship because it carried no armament. Bulloch admits, however, that he "never told any employee more than was necessary for him to know," that "everything was done quietly, without any excitement or appearance of haste." He carefully sought out and found Capt. Matthew Butcher, a British master whom he had once known as the chief officer of the Cunard steamship *Karnak.*[20]

Bulloch argues for the historical record that "no men were hired or engaged for any other purpose than that of navigating an unarmed ship, and no man was enlisted to enter the Confederate service." The catch, of course, was that many of the seamen were enlisted after the ship was afloat and out of British jurisdiction. Bulloch confided to Captain Butcher the purpose of the ship and entrusted to him the duty of turning it over safe and sound to the Confederate navy. Moreover, Bulloch's claim of innocent legality was belied by one of Dudley's spies, Clarence Randolph Yonge, who was appointed assistant paymaster of the *Alabama*. Yonge later turned over a letter from Bulloch dated July 28, 1862, appointing him as paymaster. The letter explicitly stated: "The *Alabama* may have to cruise several days in the Bristol Channel and to touch at one or two ports; during this time you are strictly enjoined not to mention that you are in any way connected with the Confederate States Navy but you will simply act as the purser of a private ship."[21]

In the middle of July, Bulloch learned that the Confederate navy department wished him to remain in England to supervise the building of more warships, and that Capt. Raphael Semmes, the Confederacy's most famous naval officer, had been appointed to command the *Alabama*. Bulloch was disappointed, as he had hoped to command the formidable Southern raider himself.

From the very beginning of its construction, there was skillful coordination of the armaments to outfit the *Alabama* as a warship. As Bulloch describes:

> The battery was ordered very shortly after the contract for the ship was made, and all the ordnance supplies were put in train in good time; but such instructions were given as would ensure their being ready not much before the ship; although the parties contracted with were not informed for what purpose they were wanted, or even how they were to be shipped, until the time for forwarding them. The necessary number of revolvers, short rifles with cutlass bayonets, ammunition, made-up clothing for 150 men, extra stores of all kinds, hammocks, and, in fact, everything required for the complete equipment of a man-of-war, were ordered.[22]

Bulloch next purchased a barque of about 450 tons to carry the equipment and rendezvous with the *Alabama* once she had escaped. On July 26, Bulloch received "information from a private but most reliable source, that it would not be safe to leave the 290 in Liverpool another forty-eight hours." The Confederate commander hastily made preparations for the escape on Monday, July 28. "None of the crew were given an inkling of the contemplated movement; but I informed Captain Butcher confidentially that the ship would not return, and directed him to get on board some extra tons of coal, to complete his stores." [23]

On Tuesday the twenty-ninth, the ship came out of its dock and anchored in the stream. The guest party of Confederate sympathizers was welcomed aboard, and in the company of the tug *Hercules*, the 290 cruised at an average speed of 12.8 knots and proceeded out to sea. At four that afternoon,

Bulloch and his guests disembarked to the *Hercules,* and the *Alabama* sailed on to an anchorage off the Welsh coast. On the next day, July 30, Bulloch again boarded the tug *Hercules,* carrying last-minute supplies and crew members recruited by a British shipping master.

The British seamen were accompanied by a comparable number of women, who Bulloch informed the shipmaster would not be permitted aboard the ship. But the women (the record does not state whether they were wives, girlfriends, or prostitutes, but undoubtedly all were represented) would not part from the seamen unless they received the men's first month's pay in advance. As a result, Captain Bulloch, the final supplies, thirty-five or forty seamen, and their women all went out in the tug to the *Alabama.* Bulloch ordered a substantial supper for the new crew and their ladies, then called the men aft and asked if they would ship for a run to Havana and intermediate ports. If the ship did not return to England, Bulloch promised to send the men back free of expense or compensate them for such a return. He agreed to give them one month's pay in advance, which would be turned over to the women. All but two or three of the sailors signed up, and the women then departed on the tugboat.[24]

Thomas Dudley kept a careful watch on the 290 while awaiting some action by the British authorities to stop it. On the thirtieth, one of Dudley's agents reported that the *Hercules* was taking additional equipment and crew members out to the 290, which was waiting off the northern coast of Wales; that she had taken on gunpowder during the night; and that six guns had been hidden below deck. The last two statements were incorrect. Bulloch was too astute to arm the ship in British territory. Dudley sent an immediate telegram to Adams and called upon the customs collector to investigate these facts. The collector found nothing "which would justify further action." The next day, the collector was ordered to seize the Confederate warship and examine the captain of the tugboat. It was too late. The *Alabama* had already put out to sea.

The Liverpool consul continued his tenacious struggle to prevent the escape of the *Alabama* to the very end. On the day the Southern raider put to sea off the coast of Wales, Dudley sent a letter describing the escape of the *Alabama* to thirty-five American consuls and to the American ministers in the major European capitals. He asked each to inform the American government if the ship should appear in his area and to aid in the prevention of her arming as a Confederate raider. In addition, he had recruited a spy who signed on as the paymaster of the *Alabama.*

Douglas Maynard, who has carefully researched the escape of the *Alabama,* describes the denouement:

In continuation of desperation measures, a detective was sent to Holyhead on August 2 to look for the 290, and an advance paynote of one of the crew members was purchased for 2 pounds and ten shillings in hopes that it would provide incriminating evidence against the persons connected with the ship. A few days later a merchant ship, the *Bahama,* was observed taking on guns and ammunition, and at the time of her departure with extra sailors on board, it was correctly surmised that she was destined to rendezvous with the Confederate gunboat.

When the *Bahama* returned to Liverpool, depositions were obtained from two seamen, one who had gone out on the 290, the other on the *Bahama,* detailing the movements of the warship from the time of her escape to her arming and commissioning in the Azores. These and affidavits concerning the *Alabama* obtained in later months were submitted to Lord Russell for the purpose of completing the record and bolstering, for future use, the American claims against Great Britain.[25]

Charles Francis Adams, in an effort to take all necessary measures to stop the *Alabama,* had requested in June that Seward order the *Tuscarora,* a Union warship, to European waters to intercept the *Alabama,* if she should escape. Adams ordered the *Tuscarora's* captain, Tunis A. Craven, to take whatever measures were necessary to intercept the *Alabama* on the way out. When Dudley informed the London legation that the *Alabama* was already out on the Mersey River, Craven sailed the *Tuscarora* out of Southampton and into St. George's Channel between Wales and Ireland in search of the *Alabama.* But when the *Tuscarora* arrived, the *Alabama* had already departed.

Bulloch reports in his memoirs that he was aware of the presence of the *Tuscarora* in British waters, and that because of the "nervous apprehension" of the U.S. consul in relation to the *Alabama,* "it did not require much acumen to connect the presence of the *Tuscarora* in British waters with the supposed character and probable destination" of the *Alabama.* "Arrangements were made with a judicious friend at Southampton to keep me informed of the *Tuscarora's* movements, and I had received almost daily advices."[26]

Bulloch advised Captain Butcher to sail the *Alabama* out to sea by the North Channel, and the *Tuscarora* never discovered her. Minister Adams was very displeased with Craven and his bungled attempt to find the *Alabama,* just as Bulloch was pleased with his own deception. Bulloch comments: "Means were adopted to mislead Captain Craven, who I must say, has proved himself to be a very credulous officer, as well as a very rude man. He went prying about in the harbors and bays of the Irish and English coast long after the *Alabama* was fairly off."[27]

Benjamin Moran, secretary of the U.S. legation in London, was quick to assess the blame for the outrageous escape of the Confederate cruiser. He wrote in his journal on August 2, "Indifference and connivance characterized the entire proceedings of H.M. officers in this matter, and Edwards, the Collector at L'pool, has aided her escape by falsehood and perjury."[28] A month later, in correspondence with Dudley, he noted that Edwards "must be a great scamp."

The *Alabama* made its rendezvous in the Azores with two ships sent by Bulloch to supply it, the *Bahama* and the *Agrippina*. Bulloch sailed together with Commander Semmes in the *Bahama,* and they arrived at Terceira in the Azores and anchored at Praya Bay on August 20. By the twenty-second, Bulloch reports, "the last gun of the battery was mounted, the powder and shell all stowed, shot in their racks." The Confederate flag was hoisted with three cheers from the crew, and the *Alabama* was ready for a prolonged and devastating cruise against Northern shipping.[29]

Secretary of State Seward was angry at the British for allowing the *Florida* and *Alabama* to escape and threatened to loose Northern privateers against British ships in retaliation, but Congress refused to support the idea. Secretary of the Navy Gideon Welles, however, gave the impetuous Capt. Charles Wilkes of *Trent* fame commission of a U.S. warship to hunt down the two Confederate cruisers. Nothing came of this assignment; the two raiders would meet their fates by other hands.

Bulloch was naturally elated by his success in outwitting such determined adversaries as Dudley, Wilding, and Adams. But the diplomatic and intelligence campaign launched by Adams and Dudley against Bulloch's shipbuilding operation was soon to reap its own rewards. Lord Palmerston and Lord Russell were now forced to take into account the dangers for England in a policy that tilted too far in favor of the Confederate South. Russell was subsequently forced to admit to Adams that the escape of the *Alabama* had been a scandal, but similar scandals involving British official support for the Confederate states continued throughout the war.

CHAPTER 5

The Pirates at Work

THE FIRST CONFEDERATE GUNBOAT BUILT IN BRITISH SHIPYARDS, THE *ORETO*, had successfully escaped and set sail directly for Nassau. On reaching that port, she was seized upon complaint of the American consul but was subsequently released by the British Admiralty Court because she was unarmed. The arms, however, were resting securely in the *Bahama*, the ship Bulloch had arranged to meet the *Oreto* in the West Indies. Transfer of the guns and ammunition took place at a small coral island seventy-five miles south of Nassau. On August 17, 1862, the *Oreto*, having been renamed the *Florida*, raised the Confederate flag and set sail for Cuba.[1]

Her commander, John Newland Maffitt, had entered the U.S. Navy at the age of thirteen as a midshipman and, after many years of service in the navy, resigned at the beginning of the Civil War to serve the South. Bulloch enthusiastically recommended him to the Confederate government for command of the first British-built steam-powered Southern warship.

The cruise of the *Florida* began disastrously when the crew, including the captain, came down with yellow fever. Captain Maffitt's stepson and three other crew members died, forcing the ship to put into Cárdenas, Cuba, where the dead were buried. Aware that the Northern fleet was looking for him, Maffitt decided to run his ship through the blockade into Mobile. Ill and feverish, Maffitt and his sick crew faced a nightmarish voyage when it was discovered that the *Florida's* guns were inoperable because the ship had not been equipped with rammers, sponges, sights, and elevating screws.

On the approach to Mobile Bay, the Confederates discovered that the port was guarded by two Union warships: the *Oneida* and the *Winona*. Nevertheless, Maffitt made the decision to run the gauntlet with his defenseless ship. Desperately ill, the captain had to be carried on deck to command the operation. He later recorded his recollection of the famous dash to Mobile:

> When quite near the *Oneida* I was hailed and ordered to heave to immediately. . . . I declined to obey the order, and immediately received a broadside, the effect of which was to carry away all my hammock nettings and much of my standing and running rigging. The superior speed of the *Florida* enabled me to pass the *Oneida*. She continued her bombardment. One 11-inch shell passed through the coal bunkers on the port-side, struck the port forward boiler, took off one man's head as it passed on the berth deck, wounding nine men. If it had exploded, which it failed to do, I no doubt would have lost every man in the vessel except the two men at the helm, as I had ordered all the crew below. Immediately after this a shot from the *Winona* entered the cabin and passed through the pantry; an 11-inch shell from the *Oneida* exploded closer to the port gangway and seriously wounded the vessel. . . . Several men were wounded in the rigging, the sheets and tyes shot away, so that I was not enabled to set the sails properly. At this moment I hauled down the English flag, under which I was sailing as ruse de guerre, and gave the order to one of the helmsmen to hoist the Confederate flag. At that moment he lost his finger with a shrapnel shot, so that my order in regard to the flag could not be complied with. . . . When we anchored under the guns of Fort Morgan shortly after sundown, the *Florida* was a perfect wreck, and only succeeded in escaping by the smoothness of the sea and her superior speed.[2]

During the three and a half months it took to rebuild the *Florida,* more of the crew died of yellow fever. Despite these hardships, the ship was successfully repaired while Maffitt recruited a new crew, including the most able officers in the Confederate navy. The Confederate commander then made a daring night run through the blockade to begin the *Florida*'s career as the scourge of Northern shipping. In the meantime, the *Alabama* was already at work setting fire to the Yankee merchant fleet.

Following the escape of the *Alabama* through the North Channel into the Irish Sea, Bulloch was put ashore in Ireland. He promptly returned to Liverpool to organize the loading of arms and ammunition for the *Alabama* on the steamer *Agrippina*. Bulloch then sailed on the *Bahama* together with Captain Semmes. On August 20, 1862, they reached the Azores, where they supervised the arming of the new Confederate cruiser. Bulloch reported to Stephen Mallory, secretary of the Confederate navy:

> On Sunday morning (the 24th), the *Alabama* and *Bahama* steamed slowly off the land, and when beyond the marine league which was covered by the jurisdiction of Portugal, our own national colors were hoisted for the first time at the *Alabama*'s peak, welcomed by three cheers from the united crews of both vessels. Now came the business of shipping the men formally for the Confederate States service, making out their allotment tickets, arranging their accounts, etc. This could be done leisurely, for we were on the high seas, beyond the reach of Foreign Enlistment Acts and Neutrality Proclamations, the most annoying foes we have to contend with on this side of the Atlantic.

"After bidding Captain Semmes a cordial adieu," Bulloch stepped over the *Alabama*'s side at midnight.[3]

What Bulloch did not know was that Thomas Dudley's intelligence operation was uncovering all that the Confederate agent hoped to keep secret. In addition, Dudley had recruited a spy, Clarence Yonge, who was now serving as paymaster aboard the *Alabama*. On September 2, the Liverpool consul sent a dispatch to Secretary of State Seward, telling him: "The steamer *Bahama* returned to this port yesterday. You will see by the enclosed slips from the newspapers of this day that my information that she was taking a part of the armaments and crew to the Gunboat 290 was correct. The 290 is now called the *Alabama* and has entered her cruise with Captain Semmes late of the *Sumter* as Commander. There is much rejoicing over this news among those who sympathize with the Rebels."[4]

Dudley informed Seward that a man named Edwin Haigh claimed to own the *Bahama*, although the *Bahama, Bermuda, Julia Usher,* and a number of other blockade runners were actually owned by the firm of Fraser, Trenholm "who act as the agents of the Rebel Government. You will observe that they have no vessels in their own names, the reason for this is that all the members of this firm with the exception of Mr. Armstrong, who has very recently been admitted, are citizens of the United States."[5]

The next day, Dudley sent another dispatch to Seward, enclosing an affidavit of a boatswain mate who shipped out on the *Alabama,* with a bill for his services signed by Captain Butcher. "He returned on the Bahama. He states that the Alabama is to cruise on the line of packets from Liverpool to New York, that Semmes told him so, this may have been said for the purpose of misleading us."[6] Dudley was proving to be an astute intelligence operator who clearly understood the tactics of disinformation. In the months ahead, however, Captain Semmes showed a remarkable capacity to elude the pursuit of the Federal navy, which searched for him in vain.

Raphael Semmes, who was soon to gain fame as the most renowned Southern naval commander of the war, had been appointed as a midshipman in the U.S. Navy in 1826, had served on many ships, and had seen action during the Mexican War. During his time at sea, he spent long hours studying law, meteorology, navigation, oceanography, and literature. After the Mexican War, he settled in Mobile, where he practiced law and wrote a book about his war experience.

In February 1861, at the age of fifty-two, Semmes resigned from the U.S. Navy and reported personally to the new Confederate president, Jefferson Davis, who assigned him the task of purchasing war supplies for the South. Semmes traveled to New York, where he hired skilled mechanics experienced in the manufacture of ordnance, purchased large quantities of percussion caps, and made contracts for the delivery to the South of powder, batteries of light artillery, and machinery for rifling cannons.

He returned to the South on April 22 to take command of the *Habana*, a passenger steamer plying between New Orleans and Cuba. Semmes found the vessel "only a dismantled packet ship, full of upper cabins, and other top hamper, furniture and crockery, but as unlike a ship of war as possible. Still I was pleased with her general appearance. Her lines were easy and graceful, and she had a sort of saucy air about her, which seemed to say, that she was not averse to the service on which she was about to be employed."[7]

Semmes supervised the transformation of this passenger steamer into the first formidable Southern cruiser, soon to be commissioned as the *Sumter*. The ship was stripped down to deck level then rebuilt and armed with an eight-inch shell gun "pivoted amidships and four light 32-pounders . . . each in broadside." After a bold run through the Federal blockade, Semmes hoisted the Confederate flag and began his career as the most daring pirate of the South.

Tall and slender, Semmes sported a tuft of beard on his lower lip and a dashing mustache twisted to needle points at the tips. His men called him "Old Beeswax." He maintained a bellicose loyalty to the Confederacy and the system of slavery to the end of his life.

On July 3, 1861, while cruising off the Yucatán coast, the *Sumter* came across her first prize. As Semmes described it, "The doomed ship was from the Black Republican State of Maine." Bearing the name of the *Golden Rocket*, it "was a fine bark, nearly new, of about seven hundred tons, and was seeking in ballast, a cargo of sugar in some one of the Cuban ports." Semmes dispatched a boat to take off the crew, sails, paint, and whatever else proved to be valuable on the ship. At ten o'clock at night, the order was given to burn the captured Yankee vessel.

Semmes's description of the torching of the *Golden Rocket* is worth quoting at length since the same action would be repeated scores of times as the *Sumter, Florida, Alabama,* and other Confederate raiders swept the seas of Northern commercial ships during the entire course of the Civil War.

Suddenly, one of the crew exclaimed, "There is the flame! She is on fire!" The decks of the Maine-built ship were of pine, caulked with old-fashioned oakum, and paid with pitch; the woodwork of the cabin was like so much tinder, having been seasoned by many voyages to the tropics, and the forecastle was stowed with paints and oils. The consequence was that the flame was not long kindling, but leaped full grown, into the air, in a very few minutes after its first faint glimmer had been seen. . . . The burning ship, with the *Sumter's* boat in the act of shoving off from her side; the *Sumter* herself, with her grim, black sides, lying in repose like some great sea-monster, gloating upon the spectacle, and the sleeping sea, for there was scarce a ripple upon the water, were all brilliantly lighted. The indraught into the burning ship's holds, and cabins, added every moment new fury to the flames, and now they could be heard roaring like the fires of a hundred furnaces, in full blast. . . . The forked tongues of the devouring element, leaping into the rigging, newly tarred, ran rapidly up the shrouds, first into the tops, then to the topmast-heads, thence to the top-gallant, and royal mast heads, and in a moment more to the trucks; and whilst this rapid ascent of the main current of fire was going on, other currents had run out upon the yards, and ignited all the sails. A top-gallant sail, all on fire, would now fly off from the yard, and sailing leisurely in the direction of the light breeze that was fanning, rather than blowing, break into bright, and sparkling patches of flame, and settle, or rather silt into the sea. The yard would then follow, and being wholly submerged by its descent into the sea, would retain a portion of its flame and continue to burn, as a floating brand for some minutes. At one time, the intricate network of the cordage of the burning ship was traced, as with a pencil of fire, upon the black sky beyond, the many threads of flame twisting, and writhing, like so many serpents, that had received their death wounds. The mizzen-mast now went by the board, then the fore-mast, and in a few minutes afterward, the great main-mast tottered, reeling, and fell over the ship's side into the sea, making a noise like that of the sturdy oak of the forests when it falls by the stroke of the axeman.[8]

Semmes's conclusion to his description of the burning of an unarmed merchant ship attempts a romantic rationalization of the act: "By the light of this flambeau upon the lonely and silent sea, lighted of the passions of bad men who should have been our brothers, the Sumter, having aroused herself from her dream of vengeance, and run up her boats, moved forward on her course."[9] While Lincoln, Seward, Adams, and Dudley continued to refer to the commanders of the *Florida* and *Alabama* as "pirates," Semmes considered himself the legitimate naval commander of a ship commissioned by a sovereign nation, with his own role the equivalent of the great Revolutionary War hero John Paul Jones.

Typical of the feudal military class of the slaveowning South, Semmes considered himself a gentleman following a traditional code of honor. He prided himself on his treatment of captured prisoners. "The captain was invited to mess in the wardroom, and when he was afterwards landed, the officers generously made him up a purse to supply his immediate necessities. The crew was put into a mess by themselves, with their own cook, and was put on a footing, with regard to rations, with the Sumter's own men. We were making war upon the enemy's commerce, but not upon his unarmed seamen."[10] This practice was altered less than a year later, when Semmes as commander of the *Alabama* put captured officers and crew members in irons in retaliation for the arrest and handcuffing of officers from the *Sumter* by the Union consul in Algiers.

James Bulloch, on the other hand, lacked Semmes's enthusiasm for the work of piracy. In his memoirs, he wrote: "There can be no doubt that the destruction of unarmed and peaceful merchant ships, while quietly pursuing their voyages on the high seas, is a practice not defensible upon the principles of moral law; and it does not in these modern times harmonize with the general sentiments of commercial nations." However, he argued, "when two nations unhappily fall out and go to war, the government of each does its best to inflict the greatest amount of injury upon the other on the principle that the more burdensome and afflicting the state of war can be made to the opposing party, the more quickly will he consent to terms of peace."[11] Unfortunately for the South, Grant and Sherman followed the same pragmatic doctrine.

The *Sumter* had a short but successful cruise. After capturing eighteen ships and burning seven of them, the Confederate raider put into Gibraltar for repairs in January 1862, was bottled up by three Union warships waiting outside the harbor, and was then sold to the British, who used it as a blockade runner.

When Semmes took command of the *Alabama,* anchored in a harbor of the Azores, at the end of August 1862, he found a ship of about nine hundred tons, 230 feet in length, 32 feet in breadth, drawing 15 feet of water when fully loaded. The ship was equipped with a three-hundred-horsepower engine. He described the ship as of "the most perfect symmetry," continuing:

> She sat upon the water with a lightness and grace of a swan. She was barkentine rigged, with long lower masts, which enabled her to carry large fore-and-aft sails, as jib and try sails, which are of so much importance to a steamer, in so many emergencies. Her sticks were of the best yellow pine, that would bend in a gale, like a willow wand, without breaking and her rigging was of the best Swedish iron wire. The scantling of the vessel was light, compared with vessels of her class in the Federal Navy, but this was scarcely a disadvantage, as she was designed as a scourge of the enemy's commerce, rather than for battle.[12]

In fact, the *Alabama* was crafted for piracy and the capture of unarmed merchantmen.

Semmes noted the ingenious design combining the best attributes of steamer and sailing vessel:

> [The] *Alabama* was so constructed, that in fifteen minutes, her propeller could be detached from the shaft, and lifted in a well contrived for the purpose, sufficiently high out of the water, not to be an impediment to her speed. When this was done, and her sails spread, she was, to all intents and purposes, a sailing ship. On the other hand, when I desired to use her as a steamer, I had only to start the fires, lower the propeller, and if the wind was adverse, brace her yards to the wind, and the conversion was complete.[13]

The Confederate commander claimed that the speed of the *Alabama* was "always greatly over-rated by the enemy. She was ordinarily about a ten-knot ship." The *Alabama* mounted eight guns, consisting of six 32-pounders in broadside and two pivot guns amidships, and carried a crew of about 120 men, including 24 officers.

Once the ship had been armed, Semmes called together the crew—a heterogeneous group of English, Dutch, Irish, French, Italian, and Spanish sailors—to inform them that they were all released from the contracts under which they had sailed from Liverpool. After promising them free passage back to that port, he launched into a speech giving a Southern viewpoint on the history of the American Civil War, of which he argued that they understood little. He explained "the individual advantages which they might expect to reap from enlistment with me. The cruise would be one of excitement and adventure. We had a fine ship under us; one they might fall in love with, as they would with their sweethearts about Wapping."

"As I spoke of good pay, and payment in gold, 'hear-hear' came up from several voices. I could give them about double the ordinary wages, to compensate them for the risks they would have to run, and I promised them, in case they should be successful, 'lots of prize money,' to be voted to them by the Confederate Congress, for the ships of the enemy they would be obliged to destroy." After his description of the rewards of piracy, Semmes recruited about eighty of the ninety sailors on hand, was forced to admit that it was the finances that won them over, "and felt very relieved in consequence."[14] The *Alabama* then set out with its crew of Confederate officers and foreign mercenaries to raid the Yankee whaling fleet operating in the Azores.

On the afternoon of September 4, the *Alabama* came upon a Yankee whaler, the *Ocmulgee* of Edgartown, Massachusetts, lying to off the coast of Pico and Fayal. Semmes disguised his approach by hoisting the U.S. colors, and "the surprise," as he recalls it, "was perfect and complete." The Confederate commander professed contempt for the U.S. Navy because it failed to protect its whaling fleet and thus abandoned these ships to their fate. He removed the crew of thirty-seven from the *Ocmulgee,* taking them aboard the *Alabama* as prisoners. After burning the whaler, he released his captives in their own whaling boats.

In the following weeks, Semmes put the fear of God into his unruly crew by reading them the Articles of War, which provided the death penalty for infractions of rules. It was now clear to each sailor, according to Semmes, that "he had gotten on board a ship of war, instead of a privateer he had supposed the Alabama to be, and that he would have to toe a pretty straight mark. It is with a disorderly crew, as with other things, the first blows are the most effective. I had around me a large staff of excellent officers, who always wore side arms, and pistols, when on duty, and from this time onward we never had any trouble keeping the most desperate and turbulent characters in subjection."[15] As Semmes puts it, "The willing and obedient were treated with humanity and kindness; the turbulent were jerked down, with a strong hand, and made submissive to discipline."[16]

Sailing off the western Azores, the *Alabama,* disguising itself under the British flag, came upon the U.S. merchant ship *Starlight.* Semmes fired a warning shot across the bow of the Yankee ship, sent a prize crew aboard, and released his prisoners at the town of Santa Cruz. Among the papers confiscated from the *Starlight* were dispatches from the American consul at Fayal to Secretary of State Seward, "in which," according to Semmes, "there was the usual amount of stale nonsense about 'rebel privateers,' and 'pirates.'" In the next few weeks, the *Alabama* devastated the New England whaling fleet by capturing and burning the *Starlight, Ocean Rover, Alert, Weather Gauge, Virginia,* and *Elijah Dunbar.* Smoke from the burning whale oil blackened the skies over the Azores.

Since the whaling season was drawing to an end, Semmes began a cruise in the Gulf Stream, where, off the banks of Newfoundland, he captured the *Brilliant,* a ship from New York carrying flour and grain. Captain Semmes remarks that the "ship made a brilliant bonfire, lighting up the Gulf Stream, for many miles around." On October 7, the *Alabama* captured and burned another New England ship carrying grain to Britain. Two more ships went up in flames before the raider was caught in a hurricane, which it weathered without major damage. The Union paid dearly for British collusion in allowing the escape of the *Alabama.* In six weeks, the Confederate raider had captured and burned seventeen ships.

Captain Semmes was often amused to read denunciations of piracy against himself and his raider printed in the Northern newspapers he confiscated from captured Yankee vessels. Possessing the ideology of the Southern military class, Semmes had a profound contempt for New Englanders, considering them to be hypocrites on the question of slavery, sharp money traders, and men lacking the manners of Southern gentlemen. Officers of the Confederacy found much in common with the British aristocracy who throughout the war granted Confederate officers extended hospitality in London and the West Indies. Raphael Semmes, the Old South commander, and Thomas Haines Dudley, the Quaker lawyer from New Jersey, clearly reflected the colliding worldviews of the two separate social orders fighting for supremacy on the North American continent.

Burning ships freely as he proceeded down the East Coast, Semmes put all his prisoners aboard the brig *Baron de Castigne* and "sent her into New York." The Rebel commander exclaims, "The more the enemy abused me, the more I felt complimented." He records in his memoirs, "New York was all agog when the Baron arrived, and there was other racing and chasing after the 'pirate,' as I afterwards learned."

Since the *Alabama* was running out of coal, Semmes ordered the ship to proceed to Martinique, where he had arranged with Bulloch to rendezvous with his supply ship, the *Agrippina*. On the way to Martinique, he filled out his crew with recruits off more captured ships. Soon after the *Alabama* set anchor in the Martinique harbor, a mutiny of drunken sailors broke out on the ship. Semmes personally put down the mutiny by dousing the intoxicated seamen with buckets of seawater and putting the worst offenders in irons.[17]

While still at anchor, the *Alabama* suddenly found itself sharing the harbor with a U.S. warship that had just put into Martinique. It turned out to be the *San Jacinto*, famous for its role in the *Trent* affair. The larger Federal warship was more heavily armed than the *Alabama,* and Semmes determined to avoid a fight. He escaped in a night rain, coaled his ship off the coast of Venezuela, and then sailed off for the Gulf of Mexico, where he intended to "strike a blow at Banks' expedition which was then fitting out for the invasion of Texas."

Semmes had learned from Northern newspapers that a large expeditionary army with artillery and cavalry was being dispatched from Boston and New York to land at Galveston, which had recently been captured by Union forces. His plan was for the *Alabama* to sink a number of transport ships in the invasion force. Since it was November, and the invasion fleet was not due until January, Semmes resolved to devote the interval to a cruise off the coast of Puerto Rico, where he might waylay Yankee ships carrying gold from California.

After putting the torch to a bark from Boston, Semmes moralized on the spectacle of the burning Yankee ship:

> Sixty years before, the negro had cut the throat of the white man, ravished his wife and daughters, and burned his dwellings in the island of San Domingo, now in sight. The white man, in another country, was now inciting the negro to the perpetuation of the same crimes against another white man, whom he called brother. The white man who was thus inciting the negro, was the Puritan of New England, whose burning ship was lighting up the shores of St. Domingo. That Puritan, only a generation before, had entered into a solemn league and covenant, to restore to the Southern man his fugitive slave, if he should escape into his territory. This was the way in which he was keeping his plighted faith! Does anyone wonder that the *Alabama* burned New England ships?[18]

Sinking unarmed merchant ships was thus justified in terms of the slaveholders' creed.

Not having encountered any of the California gold steamers, the *Alabama* cruised the West Indies and then sailed to the coast of Yucatán in the Gulf, where it once again made a rendezvous with its coal tender, the *Agrippina.* The *Alabama* spent Christmas anchored off the Arcas Islands. While there, some of the Confederate officers, having learned of Lincoln's Emancipation Proclamation, made a tombstone from a large board about four feet long and two feet wide, which they placed in the most prominent spot on the nearest island. Painted in black letters on a white background, the epitaph read: "In memory of Abraham Lincoln, President of the late United States, who died of nigger on the brain, 1st January 1863." A paper was attached saying in Spanish, "Will the finder kindly favor me by forwarding this tablet to the United States' Consul at the first port he touches at."[19]

The *Alabama* arrived off the Galveston lighthouse on January 11 to discover that Confederate forces had recaptured the port while five Federal warships were engaged in shelling the city. When one of the Federal ships sailed out to investigate the *Alabama,* Semmes sailed his ship slowly along the coast, drawing the U.S. Navy warship away from its fleet. As soon as night fell, Semmes beat to quarters, ordered his crew to man the guns, and turned on the pursuing warship. Semmes quickly engaged the USS *Hatteras,* an awkward, 210-foot ironside converted wheel steamer armed with five guns, but no match for the *Alabama.*

As shells from the Confederate cruiser smashed into the engine room of the Federal gunboat, she soon began to sink. The captain of the *Hatteras* promptly surrendered, and the battle was over in thirteen minutes. This was the only Federal warship to be sunk at sea by the Confederate navy during the entire course of the war. Although the *Alabama* had been struck by five shells from the *Hatteras,* she was not seriously damaged, and only one crew member was injured. Two men on the *Hatteras* were killed and five wounded. Semmes picked up 103 survivors, put them in irons as prisoners of war, and took them to Port Royal, Jamaica, where they were released.[20]

While the *Alabama* was anchored at Port Royal, Commander Semmes took the opportunity to tour Jamaica. He lunched with British merchants and noted that "much of the magnificence of the Kingston of former days is passing away." In particular, the Rebel commander was displeased with the emancipated slaves he observed. The former slave "was the pet of the government for years after his emancipation, and English fanatics have devoted their lives to his regeneration, but all without success. He is, today, with a few exceptions about the towns, the same savage that he is in his native Dahomey . . . far below his former level of slave."[21]

Semmes displayed little more respect for the sailors making up his crew than for slaves. On returning to his ship in Kingston Harbor, he found a number of the crew drunk. He fired his paymaster, Clarence Yonge, for drunkenness and neglect of duty. Unaware that Yonge was acting as a spy for Thomas Dudley, Semmes recalls that Yonge was "hail fellow well met [comradely] with all the common sailors, and seemed to have a special fancy for the sailors of the enemy." The Rebel commander particularly detested Yonge for his marriage to a black woman in Jamaica.[22]

After being dismissed from the *Alabama,* Clarence Yonge made his way to Liverpool, where he worked closely with Thomas Dudley and Charles Adams providing testimony on the *Alabama* and the Confederate shipbuilding program in Britain. Dudley obtained valuable papers covering the cruise of the *Alabama* from Yonge's Jamaican wife and used this information as evidence in British courts.

While the *Alabama* was still in Jamaican waters, the *Florida* made a daring run through the blockade in Mobile Bay. Captain Maffitt sailed his ship out through a Yankee fleet that was waiting for him on the misty morning of January 16. Somehow the lookouts on a number of Union warships missed the *Florida* in the fog, and when the Confederate raider was finally discovered and chased by the Yankee fleet, Maffitt outsailed them and escaped.

Three days later, the *Florida* captured its first prize, a brig from Boston. After recoaling in Nassau, the *Florida* captured and burned a number of other Yankee merchantmen. In the middle of February, the *Florida* set fire to the *Jacob Bell,* a clipper ship from Boston with a cargo worth $2 million. A month later, Maffitt seized a bark from Boston and began his successful practice of converting captured ships into new Confederate raiders. He placed a lieutenant and eighteen sailors on the ship, armed it with two howitzers, and commissioned the ship to act as an independent raider. As Philip Van Doren Stern notes in his history of the Confederate navy: "The *Florida* was breeding offspring that were to be almost as dangerous as she was herself."[23]

While the *Florida* and *Alabama* continued their devastating raids on U.S. merchant ships, Thomas Haines Dudley began his massive files on Union ship losses, which would later be used as evidence for Federal claims against the British government. At the same time, the energetic Liverpool consul and his espionage ring uncovered an even greater Confederate threat to the Union cause: The Rebels had begun construction in the Laird shipyards in Liverpool of a new type of deadly ironclad warships, which became known as the Laird Rams. If delivered to the South, they would have the capacity to break the blockade and destroy the Federal navy.

CHAPTER 6

The Propaganda War

From the first day of his tenure in Liverpool, Thomas Haines Dudley had been thrust into the threefold task of building an intelligence network in Britain, carrying on his routine consular business, and engaging in the propaganda war for the hearts and minds of the British public in support of the Northern cause. Shortly after his arrival, in the middle of the *Trent* crisis, the new consul was invited to attend a banquet given in honor of John Bright, the radical member of Parliament who had the most consistent record as a friend of the United States and opponent of slavery. John Bright and Richard Cobden were the leaders of the reform movement in Parliament. Both believed in universal suffrage and wished to reform the English political system on the American model. In the House of Commons, they were widely known as "the two members for the United States."

At Rochdale on the night of December 4, 1861, Dudley was given a seat on the platform where Bright was scheduled to speak on the *Trent* affair and the American Civil War. Dudley recalls that a "stout gentleman" took the seat beside him and asked if he was Mr. Dudley, the U.S. consul at Liverpool. "I answered that I was, and he replied, 'My name is John Bright.' This was my introduction to Mr. Bright, and the commencement of a friendship which continued until his death."[1]

Bright told Dudley that he felt the weight of responsibility resting on him that night more heavily than ever before. England was on the verge of war with the United States, a democratic country that he admired, and Bright was deeply depressed. Dudley learned later that Bright had been abandoned by his radical colleague Richard Cobden, who had declined to enlist in Bright's support for the North at a time of national war hysteria.

After the banquet, Bright spoke for two hours in defense of the Northern cause. In his conclusion to a speech that was widely published in both Britain and the United States, Bright said:

> Now, whether the Union will be restored or not, or the South achieve an honored independence or not, I know not, and predict not. But this I think I know, that in a few years, the twenty millions of freemen in the North will be thirty or even fifty millions, a population equal to or exceeding that of this kingdom. When that time comes I pray that it may not be said among them that, in the darkest hour of their country's trials, England, the land of their fathers, looked on with icy coldness, and saw unmoved the perils and calamities of their children. As for me, I have but this to say. I am but one in this audience, and but one in the citizenship of this country; but if all other tongues are silent mine shall speak for that policy which gives hope to the bonds-men of the South, and which tends to generous thoughts, and generous words, and generous deeds between the two great nations who speak the English language, and from their origin alike are entitled to the English name.[2]

Five days after this speech, John Bright wrote to Dudley: "I am very obliged to you for your kind letter, and I shall be very happy if anything I have said shall contribute to the preservation of peace." Then Bright went on to make an astute assessment of British public opinion on the American Civil War: "There are two nations in England, the governing class and the millions who toil, the former dislike your Republic and their organs incessantly misrepresent and slander it—the latter have no ill feeling towards you, but are not altogether unaffected by the statements made to your prejudice. I hope however that out of present peril, we may see a brighter future, and a better understanding between your people and mine."[3]

Charles Francis Adams in London and Thomas Dudley in Liverpool were daily confronted with the anti-Northern hostility of the British governing classes. The conservative aristocracy in England had long held the opinion that the American republic was doomed to disintegration into separate states. They believed that the strain on the Union was too great, and that in the long run, the United States would be forced to abandon democracy and establish a traditional authoritarian government. The outbreak of civil war, the subsequent assumption of war powers by the Lincoln administration, including the temporary suspension of habeas corpus, and military rule in occupied territory all seemed to confirm conservative predictions.

However, as G. D. Lillibridge, a historian researching the impact of American democracy on Great Britain, notes: "There can be little doubt that many radicals were completely bewildered by Lincoln's insistence upon making the Union the issue at stake" in the Civil War.[4] Washington's equivocal stance on slavery was a major obstacle to the earnest propaganda efforts of Adams and Dudley to win the enthusiastic support of British citizens for the Northern cause.

The British were well aware that for decades, the Americans not only had permitted slavery in their country, but also had energetically opposed an international effort to end the slave trade at sea. As early as the Congress of Vienna in 1815, the British had worked for the approval by all nations of a declaration calling for the total abolition of "a commerce so odious and so strongly condemned by laws of religion and nature." While the U.S. government paid lip service to the principle of ending the slave trade at sea, it failed to enforce maritime measures against the slavers. Finally, in 1842, the United States joined Britain in a compromise treaty giving English and American naval ships the joint right to search potential slave carriers.

The distinguished maritime historian Samuel Elliot Morrison sums up the long-standing American hypocrisy on this subject:

> Laws of the U.S. and of almost every other Western nation declared the African slave trade to be piracy, punishable by death; but prior to the Lincoln administration, no American citizen was executed for the offense. Laws against it were either not enforced, or were so construed that traffic in human flesh was protected by the American flag.
>
> The British Navy was the only force seriously trying to suppress the trade; but successive administrations, faithful to the obsolete issue of visit and search, refused permission to the British to search American vessels. A slave ship only had to raise the "proud banner of freedom" to evade search and escape.[5]

The Confederate states lost little time in exploiting what they determined to be a propaganda advantage for their cause. They not only dispatched to Britain and France diplomats James Mason and John Slidell, whose mission had been interrupted by the *Trent* affair, but also sent a young man named Henry Hotze to lead the Rebel propaganda war for British public opinion. Hotze, born in Switzerland, had grown up in the South and became a prominent advocate of white supremacy. The young journalist possessed a great deal of charm and soon earned a reputation as an able advocate of the Southern cause in England.

Frank Owsley, in his seminal work, *King Cotton Diplomacy,* argues that the twenty-seven-year-old Henry Hotze ranked among the most able Confederate agents working abroad during the Civil War. "He showed more insight into public opinion and tendencies than did either Mason or Slidell, and his fastidiousness, his deftness, and his lightness of touch in a delicate situation were remarkable. His resourcefulness had a masterly finesse that would have done honor to Cavour or Bismarck."[6]

Hotze, like Raphael Semmes and James Bulloch, understood that the Southern slaveholder had more in common culturally with the British upper class than did the New Englander. However, the Swiss-born journalist found himself up against a number of capable Northern envoys sent abroad by Lincoln and Seward to fight the propaganda war in Europe. The most able among them was Thurlow Weed, Seward's friend and political adviser. Weed, an experienced politician and successful businessman, was, in the words of the young Henry Adams, "a complete American education in himself. His mind was naturally strong and beautifully balanced; his temper never seemed ruffled; his manners were carefully perfect in the style of benevolent simplicity, the tradition of Benjamin Franklin."[7]

Hotze suffered from the common conceit of the Southern elite, who universally underestimated their Northern opponents from Lincoln on down. He believed that Weed and the other Northerners who had been sent to England to promote the Northern cause would, because of their nasal twang and aggressive manner, turn out to be "repulsive to English taste." The Rebel propagandist, adroit in dispensing good cigars and whiskey, scored an early success in the propaganda war by his skillful cultivation of the British upper class. He was invited to write a lead editorial justifying the South's secession in the *Morning Post,* the organ representing the policies of Lord Palmerston, and by the end of April, he was contributing similar editorial columns to the *Standard* and the *Morning Herald,* which represented the opposition leader, Lord Derby.[8]

Subsequently, Henry Hotze persuaded the Confederate government to finance a paper of its own in London. On May 1, 1862, Hotze published the first number of the *Index,* a Confederate journal that never achieved a wide circulation but proved extremely effective in its influence on members of Parliament, editors, businessmen, and other members of the British elite. He recruited a number of well-known writers in the British press to make contributions to the journal. Hotze wrote to Secretary of State Judah P. Benjamin to justify the work of the *Index,* arguing that the paper had value not only as "a means of reaching public opinion but as a channel through which arguments and facts can be conveyed unofficially to the Government itself."[9] Hotze had remarkable success in recruiting pro-Southern editorialists from among some of the most prominent journalists in England.

Thus the leading Confederate propagandist in Britain was able to fill the British press with stories that emphasized the inefficiency of the Northern blockade, exaggerated Southern material resources, and proclaimed that the secession of the South was not for the purpose of retaining slavery, but was instead dedicated to establishing the independence of states having a legitimate conflict with the North. Hotze became the leading master of "king cotton" propaganda. His success led to an increase of funds from Richmond to step up his propaganda campaign in both England and France. There was no question that Hotze, like the other Confederate agents abroad who associated exclusively with the Tory upper class, assumed that the opinions of the aristocracy represented the views of the whole country.

In the spring of 1862, both Charles Francis Adams and Thomas Dudley had reason to be depressed by the anti-Northern hostility of officially promoted British public opinion. Relations between Washington and London hit a new low when proper British society became outraged by the conduct of Gen. Benjamin Butler, who had been made military governor of New Orleans after the city's capture by Adm. David Farragut's fleet.

Butler, a prominent Massachusetts lawyer and politician who had been appointed by Lincoln as a major general of volunteers, was a corpulent, cross-eyed man who sternly took on the task of governing a hostile population. He jailed contractors who declined to work for Northern forces, had a New Orleans resident hanged for tearing down the American flag, and collided with foreign consuls whom he considered pro-Confederate. But what most outraged the elite of British society was Butler's notorious "Woman Order" issued on May 15, 1862. General Order No. 28 declared:

> As the officers and soldiers of the United States have been subject to repeated insults from the women (calling themselves ladies) of New Orleans, in return for the most scrupulous non-interference and courtesy on our part, it is ordered that hereafter when any female shall, by word, gesture, or movement, insult or show contempt for any officer or soldier of the United States, she shall be regarded and held liable to be treated as a woman of the town plying her avocation.[10]

This order by the Union commander to treat well-born Southern ladies as "fallen women" brought forth all the indignation of which English Victorian society was capable, and the outcry against Yankee barbarism was led by

Lord Palmerston himself. The prime minister denounced Butler in the House of Commons by declaring:

> I am quite prepared to say that I think no man could have read the proclamation without a feeling of the deepest indignation. . . . Sir, an Englishman must blush to think that such an act has been committed by one belonging to the Anglo-Saxon race. If it had come from some barbarous race that was not within the pale of civilization, one might have regretted it, but that such an order should have been promulgated by a soldier—by one who had raised himself to the rank of general, is a subject undoubtedly of not less astonishment than pain.[11]

"Beast Butler," as he was called by Confederate propagandists, was pilloried in Parliament and press for his "gross, unmanly and brutal insult to every woman of New Orleans." Calls for mediation of the American Civil War surfaced once again. On June 12, Palmerston deepened the crisis in British-American relations by a private letter to Minister Charles Francis Adams protesting Butler's conduct in New Orleans. The prime minister asserted that he could not "express adequately the disgust which must be excited in the mind of every honorable man" at the conduct of a "general guilty of so infamous an act as to deliberately hand over the female inhabitants of a conquered city to the unbridled license of an unrestrained soldiery."[12] Adams was naturally furious, refused to recognize the note, and expressed his surprise that Palmerston was taking over the duties of the minister of foreign affairs.

Palmerston replied on the fifteenth, saying his letter was official. The American minister registered his indignation to Lord Russell over the prime minister's violation of diplomatic protocol and closed the unwelcome correspondence by a final note to Palmerston stating that he would decline to receive any more such private communications from the prime minister. This ended the affair, except that the American minister's firm rebuff to Palmerston ruptured all personal relations between the Palmerston and the Adams families. Benjamin Moran notes in his diary, "For a few days we considered things so serious as to strongly anticipate a sudden rupture of all intercourse."[13] There were many occasions during Minister Adams's tenure in London when he expected a complete break in relations between the two countries and an end to the American mission in Britain.

During the summer and fall of 1862, both England and France renewed the attempt to bring about European intervention in the American war. As cotton supplies dwindled and the British textile districts were confronted with massive unemployment, the internal debate in the British cabinet and among members of Parliament over recognition of the Confederacy reached a new height. Southern sympathizers throughout Britain began to pressure the government for recognition of the Confederacy.

In the middle of September, after the South's defeat of the Union army at the second battle of Bull Run, Palmerston, excited by the possibility of the loss by Union forces of Washington and Baltimore, wrote Russell: "If this should happen would it not be time for us to consider whether in such a state of things England and France might not address the contending parties and recommend an arrangement on the basis of separation." If the North should refuse to negotiate, then England and France could "acknowledge the independence of the South as an established fact."[14] Russell went even further and declared that whether or not the Union forces had been completely destroyed, England should "recognize the Southern states as an independent state."[15]

Although the British cabinet was divided during the secret debate on the question of intervention, Palmerston and Russell were successful in recruiting William Gladstone, chancellor of the exchequer, for the cause of intervention. Gladstone, however, soon embarrassed them by a serious public indiscretion. At a banquet in his honor at Newcastle on October 7, Gladstone gave a speech that people believed expressed the views of the cabinet, saying, "We may have our own opinions about slavery; we may be for or against the South; but there is no doubt that Jefferson Davis and the other leaders of the South have made an army; they are making, it appears a navy; and they have made what is more than either, they have made a nation."[16] The speech produced a sensational impression in the whole country and the international community. It appeared that both Gladstone and Russell were impelled to intervene in the American conflict because they wished to obtain cotton to forestall a revolution among the unemployed textile workers.

Charles Francis Adams wrote in his journal that if Gladstone represented the opinion of the cabinet, "then my term here is likely to be very short."[17] Thomas Dudley, referring to Gladstone's speech in a letter home, wrote bitterly, "It was true that the rebels were having a navy built; but it was being built by Englishmen in Great Britain and not in the South." A few days later, Dudley received a letter from John Bright, who told him that he knew nothing of "Gladstone's speech except that on the American question it is discreditable to him and calculated to do mischief. He comes of a family long connected with slavery and is now the Minister in a country where aristocracy rules and of which a Republic is necessarily hated—and I suppose he takes the color of the atmosphere in which he moves."[18]

President Lincoln had issued the first Emancipation Proclamation on September 22, and Bright, like many in Britain, responded by telling Dudley:

"The Proclamation is a grand move, not too soon, not too late in my opinion. It must have a good effect here in putting your enemies more and more in the wrong." Bright concluded his letter to Dudley by attempting to reassure him about the crisis in British-American relations: "Don't be too unhappy about English opinion—there will be a reaction—and it is what you do in America, and not what people think here that will decide the contest."[19]

Bright was correct. In the long run, Northern military victories would determine foreign response to the war. Lincoln had informed the cabinet of his intention to issue a proclamation for the emancipation of slavery as early as July 22. The whole cabinet, except Blair, approved of the idea, but Lincoln accepted Seward's advice that such a proclamation should be delayed until he could "give it to the country supported by military success." Thus Lincoln waited until the great repulse of Lee's army at Antietam to make his historic announcement.

During the summer of 1862, Lincoln was faced with a polarization of public opinion in the North on the question of slavery. Radical Republicans attacked the president for being indecisive, irresolute, and stumbling. On the other side, Northern Democrats exploited the race issue to the hilt. Antiblack riots broke out in a dozen Northern cities. British leaders all doubted whether the North had either the unity or the will to pursue the war to victory.

During these critical months when the British cabinet was debating the issues of intervention in the war and recognition of the Confederate states, Thomas Dudley learned, probably from his friend William Dayton in Paris, that the French had sent a special minister to London to propose a joint declaration by Britain and France to recognize the Confederacy and raise the blockade. Dudley immediately sent for a member of the British Parliament from Liverpool who was a close friend of Gladstone's. Dudley informed the man about the arrival of the French envoy and convinced him of the danger to British-American relations if the French minister succeeded in his mission.

Dudley told the member of Parliament that a recognition of the Southern Confederacy, or even an attempt at mediation between North and South, by European powers would mean war with the United States. Since Palmerston and Russell believed that the Democratic Party in the North, which opposed the war, might win the next election, Dudley argued that those Democrats, many of whom were foreigners, would be willing to take up arms against England, and that he himself "would go home and undertake to raise an army of five hundred thousand men in the North . . . for the pupose of invading Canada; and just as certain as the sun would rise, if England should take this step she would lose Canada and all her other British possessions in North America."[20]

Thomas Haines Dudley—
U.S. consul at Liverpool

Charles Francis Adams—
U.S. minister to England

William H. Seward—
U.S. secretary of state

James Dunwoody Bulloch—
chief of Confederate
Secret Service in Europe

Raphael Semmes—
commander,
Confederate raider *Alabama*

Lord Palmerston—
prime minister, England

Lord John Russell—
foreign minister, England

The *Florida* burns the *Jacob Bell*.

Screw steamer no. 90—the *Alabama*

The *Alabama* stops a merchant ship at sea.

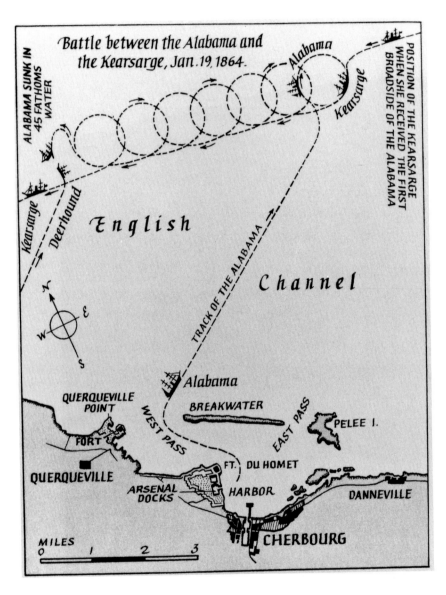

Battle courses of the *Alabama* and the *Kearsarge*

BATTLES AND LEADERS OF THE CIVIL WAR

Consternation
on the approach
of the *Alabama*.
Drawing by
Winslow Homer.

Ironclad ram

Alexandra

Shenandoah

The Liverpool consul wished the British to fully understand the consequences of a war with the United States. "Your treasury will be emptied, your business at home and abroad injured, your commerce swept from the ocean by our cruisers, and you will lose forever your possessions on the North American continent," he declared in passionate terms, saying that "it would have been impossible for the South to have carried on the conflict for one year if it had not been for the aid and assistance which they had received from England."[21]

Dudley learned, just as he had expected, that the member of Parliament took the next train to London and went directly to Mr. Gladstone's house.

> I followed him in a later train and went to the legation, where I had
> a conference with Mr. Adams, and told him what I had done. Mr.
> Adams approved of my action, and in an interview with Earl Russell
> the next day confirmed the statement that I had made. What took
> place in the English Cabinet, in their discussions upon this question,
> we have never been informed; the only thing we know is this, that
> the proposal made by the French Emperor was declined by England,
> and a bloody war was thus averted.[22]

At the same time, the Confederate commissioners, Mason and Slidell, who knew of the French plans for intervention, were convinced that cotton was, indeed, king and that European intervention was at last about to occur. Mason wrote to Benjamin on November 7, 1862: "The cotton famine . . . which has been pressing hard upon the manufacturing districts, is looming up in fearful proportions. . . . The public mind is very much agitated and disturbed at the fearful prospect for winter, and I am not without hope that it will produce its effects on the counsels of government."[23] Mason thought it unlikely that the British would turn down the French offer for joint intervention. Slidell believed that England would probably agree to joint intervention, and if not, the French would act without the British.

Modern historians who have had full access to the diplomatic archives agree that British-American relations had reached a turning point in the fall of 1862, and that the Northern display of strength at Antietam and Lincoln's Emancipation Proclamation had had an effect on the outcome of British decision making.[24] Public opinion in Britain was beginning to swing against recognition of the Confederacy and intervention in the American war.

Prime Minister Palmerston introduced the French proposal to the cabinet on November 11. Lord Russell, believing that the strong gains made by the Democratic Party in the recent congressional elections "afforded a most favorable opportunity for intervention," urged acceptance of the French proposal. Palmerston and Gladstone also came down on the side of intervention.

The key actor in this crisis, however, proved to be Sir George Cornewall Lewis, secretary for war in Palmerston's cabinet. Lewis led a campaign within the government and in the press against intervention in the war, and his cogent arguments swung both elite and public opinion to favor strict neutrality in the American conflict. The majority in the cabinet voted down the proposal for joint intervention with France sponsored by Russell, Palmerston, and Gladstone.[25]

Russell notified the French of the British rejection of their proposal and published the text of his reply to Paris in the London *Times*. But Russell's reply to the French "stressed the fact that the subject was deferred not closed. . . . It remained British policy to wait for the spring. American affairs were now 'at a standstill.'"[26]

Later in his life, the noted historian Brooks Adams, the youngest son of Charles Francis Adams, looked back at the fateful fall of 1862 and remembered it as a turning point in British-American relations. He concludes: "The English aristocracy had collapsed with the repulse of Lee at Antietam. By a subtle instinct all Europe and America became conscious of a change of status. It was the United States now which pressed upon England, not England on the United States."[27] After the fall of 1862, he notes, his father did not shrink from the use of coercive diplomacy against Russell and Palmerston. The danger of war between the two powers remained, however, as the Confederates redoubled their efforts to build a modern navy in Britain, and Confederate sympathizers continued to occupy powerful positions in the government and business.

Perhaps the most effective propagandist for the Southern cause besides Hotze was the Englishman James Spence, who wrote the most popular book on the United States ever published in England. Spence's book, *The American Union*, justified the secession of the South. Spence, a Liverpool cotton trader, although not a member of Parliament, became a leader of the most powerful group in England, which worked night and day for recognition of the Confederate states as an independent nation and for British intervention in the American Civil War. The group was made up of members of Parliament, shipowners, shipbuilders, and wealthy merchants.

Spence published *The American Union* in 1861, and by February, the book had gone through four printings. The *London Economist* believed that Spence's book had done more "to mould into definite form the floating mass of public opinion on the right and wrong doing of the Southern States in the matter of secession" than any other book on the subject. Frank Owsley explains why Spence's book had such a profound impact on the British public:

> In his book Spence had convincingly argued the sovereign nature of the American states and their constitutional right to secede. With even greater force he placed before the English the fundamental difference between the North and the South which made the secession of the South inescapable. The North was industrial, powerful, and constantly threatening the less powerful rural and agricultural South. But the thing which created the deepest impression was not so much the economic differences between the two sections as the racial. The North, according to Spence, was composed of a conglomerate, unfused mass of nationalities—Irish, German, Swiss, Swedish, Danish, Italian, Hungarian, Polish, Russian, Jewish, Romanian and Turkish—an inferior, mongrel people, while the South was almost pure British. This idea stuck and even today sticks in the British mind—and the majority of the British soon felt a racial sympathy with the South they did not have for the North.[28]

On the other hand, the British of all classes had little sympathy with slavery. Hotze himself had translated Spence's book into French and German, but apparently he and the leaders of the Confederacy had not read the book carefully. Spence realized that the British public would never accept slavery, and his book attacked slavery as "a foul blot from which all must desire to purge the annals of the age."

By 1863, Spence had been appointed as the financial agent for the Confederacy in England and was speaking in public, particularly in Liverpool, in support of the Southern cause. In late November 1863, Confederate sympathizers were complaining to Hotze that Spence was not following the Confederate line and was "making unnecessarily large concessions to the antislavery prejudice." Hotze reported these facts to Secretary of State Benjamin in Richmond. As a result, Benjamin dismissed Spence from his position as the financial agent of the South.[29] But there was little question that British public opinion was making the turn against the slaveowning South, especially after Lincoln's first Emancipation Proclamation, which went into effect on January 1, 1863.

Thomas Haines Dudley took note of all these developments in a long dispatch to Seward on January 6, 1863. Dudley informed Seward: "There are some symptoms of a change in sentiment in this country towards the United States. The abolition feeling which has lain dormant since the contest commenced shows signs of life since the issuing of the President's proclamation of the 22nd September last." Dudley reported on a number of meetings held to support Lincoln's Emancipation Proclamation, the most important of which was held in Manchester. He noted the deep feeling against slavery in England, but that "every effort has been made to keep it down. The people have been told by the leading men and the press that slavery was not involved in the question," no matter who won the war, and that "the North always had and always would continue to uphold slavery in the South. Mr. Spence in his book on the American Union which has been more extensively read in this country than any other book on the subject takes the ground that slavery will be more certainly abolished if the South succeed in establishing their independence, than if the North succeed and the union is restored."

Dudley then goes on to say that "efforts to mislead and deceive the people have been too successful. The proclamation of the 22nd of September seems to have opened their eyes and now all over the kingdom there are signs of a healthy reaction. If it once gets fairly aroused as our friends predict, it will sweep everything before it, and the papers and interested parties will not be able to smother or repress it." Dudley was beginning to evince a rare optimism about British public opinion. He concludes his report to Seward by returning to his intelligence capacity: "The Steamer Georgiana has entered to load today for Nassau. So I have been informed since the above was written. A. E. Bymer & Co. are the Consignees, her commander is M. B. Davidson."[30]

Throughout the war, the Union's Liverpool consul acted as a one-man propaganda army for the North. He corresponded with members of Parliament, wrote letters to the newspapers, printed his own pamphlets on various subjects relevant to British policy toward the United States, and distributed these to all members of the government and the press. He never lost a chance to get in a word for the cause he represented.

Dudley recalls finding himself seated next to an English admiral at a dinner given for the judges of the Court of Assizes. "During the dinner [the man] turned in a condescending manner and asked me if we had any news from the war. I answered, yes, that there had been a naval engagement, a fight between the 'Monitor' and the 'Merrimac.'" The admiral indicated that there was hardly much significance to this battle, to which the consul replied that he regarded it as "the most extraordinary naval fight that had taken place during the century." Dudley concludes, "I shall never forget the contemptuous look he gave as he turned from me."[31] Two weeks later, Dudley recalls, the *London Times* had come to understand the significance of the battle and declared that, in fact, England had no navy and her obsolete ships could not stand up to the monitors the United States was in the process of constructing.

It was among the British working classes that the strongest support came for the Northern cause. In the fall of 1862, the *New York Times* sent a correspondent to report on the effects of the "cotton famine" on the Lancashire textile workers. In a series of articles, the *Times* reported on "The Distress in Lancashire," "Terrible Effects of the Cotton Famine in England," and "Quarter of a Million of People in One District Out of Work and Living on Charity." On November 8, the *Times* carried a leading editorial headed, "Our Friends in England—A Practical Suggestion."[32]

The *Times* asserted that friends of the Union could not be found among the British rulers, aristocracy, and governing classes or the press, but only among the masses of workmen. Then the *Times* suggested that Americans send over bounty ships full of corn and wheat to aid the starving textile workers of Lancashire. The call was taken up by the American press and chambers of commerce and churches in every major city, and a vast movement of relief for the British unemployed got under way.

A new ship of eighteen hundred tons, the *George Griswold*, loaded with relief supplies, was towed out of New York on January 9, 1863, on her way to England. She carried 13,236 barrels of flour, 102 boxes of bacon, 50 barrels of pork, 500 barrels of corn, 315 boxes and 125 barrels of bread, 50 barrels of wheat, and large amounts of rice. The *Griswold* was followed by other relief ships, including the *Achilles* and the *Hope*. Thomas Dudley was responsible for receiving these ships and distributing the relief once the ships arrived in Liverpool.[33]

Philip Foner, the American labor historian who has documented the vast movement of British labor support for the North during the Civil War, records the arrival of the *Griswold* at Liverpool:

> The George Griswold tied up at Liverpool on February 11, 1863, with its provisions valued at 27,000 pounds and donations of 1,300 in cash. . . . All of the men employed at the docks, from custom officials to porters and stevedores, refused payments for their services, while the railways offered free transport. Even before the George Griswold landed at Liverpool, meetings were held in Leeds and Rochdale, attended mainly by workingmen, to express thanks to the American people for the approaching vessel.[34]

A week later, a public meeting sponsored by the Liverpool Chamber of Commerce and attended by Consul Dudley was held to officially thank Captain Lunt of the *Griswold* for the shipment of American relief supplies. Captain Lunt and the Reverend Dennison, the ship's chaplain, then traveled throughout the cotton districts, where they were welcomed by enthusiastic public meetings. On February 24, the crowd at Manchester's Free Trade Hall was so packed that another meeting of two thousand people was held outside.

According to Foner, J. R. Cooper, the chairman of the meeting, and several speakers made it clear that the occasion was a logical sequence to the great Free Trade Hall meeting of December 31, 1862, "a meeting that took place on the 'eve of a bright dawn of freedom to the negro slave.' Out of that meeting had been born the Union and Emancipation Society, under whose auspices the present gathering was being held. As the society had widely publicized both the address to President Lincoln and his reply, it was only fitting that Lincoln's reply to the workers of Manchester be read to the present gathering."[35] The final speaker at this meeting was the Chartist leader, Ernest Jones, who "pointed out that propagandists for the Confederacy had charged that the purpose of the relief ship was to 'win over' working class support for the Union. 'But,' Jones cried to wild applause, 'ere one pound's worth of food was shipped or collected, the voice of the working men of England went forth in a cry of sympathy to the North, and of ratification of the principles of liberty.'"[36]

Large numbers of British workingmen had emigrated to the United States before and during the war, and their letters home had reinforced sympathy for the North in the manufacturing districts, reflected by the fact that British shipyard workers sympathetic to the cause of the North made up a key element of Thomas Dudley's spy network in Britain. The Liverpool consul's new-found optimism in his dispatches to Seward concerning the turn in British public opinion were daily confirmed by events of the early months of 1863.

In alliance with the workers' movement opposing the Confederacy were some forty African-Americans residing in England. These included fugitive slaves from the South who were actively engaged in the campaign to win popular support for the Union cause. A number of them participated in lecture tours to describe the horrors of slavery. Their voices added to the sweeping anti-Confederate propaganda movement led by British unions and the newly established Emancipation Society.[37]

Consul Dudley was swamped with work during this time, while he kept watch on the Confederate shipbuilding projects, carried on extensive propaganda and diplomatic efforts, and singlehandedly maintained the routine work of the consulate. This last activity concerned, for a large part, controversies between American ships' officers and seamen over wages, abuse of seamen by officers, improper food, crimes and offenses committed on the high seas, and the petitions of destitute seamen.

From his first day in office, the New Jersey lawyer found himself besieged by stranded seamen who came to his office with petitions for relief. He was characteristicly consistent in his sympathy for the downtrodden, whether slaves or unemployed seamen. American sailors who either had been shipwrecked or had jumped ship because of ill treatment from officers soon exhausted the funds provided for their relief, and Dudley had to appeal to the State Department for more money. The State Department in turn demanded that Dudley reduce the expenditures for American seamen. In a remarkable letter to the secretary of state, Thomas Dudley took on the whole complex question of the manning practices of the American merchant marine.

In his long dispatch on the subject to Seward, the Liverpool consul writes:

A reply to your question how to reduce the expenditures for the relief of destitute seamen involves an enquiry into the present state of the laws with the regard to the manning of ships and the employment of seamen and the annunciation of some better system; for undoubtedly it is chiefly owing to the imperfections of the present system that so many seamen leave these vessels in foreign ports and become chargeable to the Government and there is no doubt very many shipwrecks are caused by inefficient manning and incompetent seamen.

Dudley proposed new legislation and a commission of inquiry headed by a retired sea captain to review the subject. He then attacked the whole system of shipping seamen and the way they were recruited. The consul had obviously made a careful study of the inferior quality of maritime officers and the system of kidnapping, cheating, and drugging of seafarers by shipping masters who made a profit from selling men:

The whole thing is managed by shipping masters, the master of the vessel rarely seeing the men until he goes aboard to get the ship under way and then he finds most of them helpless or stupified with drink or drugging. . . . It is then found that a large proportion of the men shipped are altogether incapable of doing seamen's duty; of those who are, most have been brought on board drunk and have been cheated out of their advances. They are in consequence sullen and discontented.

He continues: "One can imagine what must be the sort of life passed under such circumstances throughout the voyage." These victimized individuals are deprived of proper clothing and are soon reduced to "the most pitiable plight. It is not uncommon for men to arrive here shoeless and half clad offensive beyond expression from accumulated filth."

The men are "largely in arrears to the vessel for the advance paid to the shipping master so they can obtain no further advance to buy clothes and glad to escape a state of experience and intolerable misery they desert and what wonder." Dudley continues in an impassioned defense of ordinary seamen, with no redress for their abuse by brutal officers. He finally spells out a detailed reform program for the whole system, proposing that "seamen's contracts be voluntarily and legally made and rigidly enforced" and calling for "licensing of shipping masters who have no interest in deception and would be responsible to the seamen and ship for his conduct." A training program would be established for boys on ships, and navigation schools set up in every port. "There are in all our Atlantic cities a large number of vagabond boys and youths many of whom are under the present system frequently shipped off as seamen. They are abused and plundered in the way before stated and in turn they themselves become inured to like practices." Dudley argues that if "they could receive a year's training they would make honest and valuable seamen."

In addition, the Quaker consul proposed a new system of relief for sick seamen, including seamen's hospitals, since the cause for so many desertions was that "the master would not agree to seek medical help for sick seamen." It was for this reason that the expenses for sick seamen and deserters continued to fall on the consulate in Liverpool. Finally, Dudley proposed new treaties with foreign powers for the arrest of deserters and the prompt punishment of officers on shipboard. The secretary of state had written Dudley to reduce relief expenditures for seamen but had received in return an eighteen-page reply detailing the reformation of the entire manning program of the American commercial fleet. Lincoln's agent in Liverpool was something more than a chief of espionage.[38]

Still, Dudley's operation against the Confederacy in Britain continued in full force. By the end of 1862, he was taking depositions of captains who had been captured and had their ships burned by the *Alabama*. Dudley was building his files for legal claims against Great Britain. In the meantime, he had discovered the construction of two new and deadly armored warships with which the Confederates hoped to sink the Federal navy and break the blockade. As Philip Van Doren Stern notes, "Dudley kept himself so well posted about the building of the two ironclad rams that he was almost as familiar with their progress as Bulloch was."[39] The struggle over these new Confederate ships would once again bring Washington and London to the brink of war.

CHAPTER 7

The Confederate Rams

James Dunwoody Bulloch set himself the task of building Confederate warships in Britain that would be superior to any ship in the rapidly growing Federal navy. In July 1862, Bulloch signed a contract with the Laird shipyard for construction of two ironclads that would be better armored and possess more firepower than the Federal navy could match. The two vessels, to be named the *North Carolina* and the *Mississippi*, but known in the Laird yards as nos. 294 and 295, were designed to mount four nine-inch rifles on revolving turrets. They were called rams because they possessed formidable, seven-foot underwater rams capable of sinking most Federal warships. Bulloch believed that his ironclads would be invincible and suggested to Mallory that once out of England, they could be used to break the Federal blockade, steam up the Potomac to "render Washington untenable," and then sail up to Portsmouth, New Hampshire, where they would destroy the Federal navy yard.[1]

Thomas Dudley kept a close surveillance on every step in the construction of these potentially deadly additions to the Confederate navy. On August 30, Dudley reported to Seward and Adams that the keel of no. 294 had been laid in the stocks of the *Alabama*. In addition to these warships, Dudley's agents reported that Bulloch had made another contract with William Miller and Sons for the construction of a screw steamer designed as a raider. This ship was called the *Alexandra*. The Liverpool consul informed Seward that armored plates for the new Rebel ironclads were being produced by Mersey Steel and Ironworks. They were four-and-three-quarter-inch-thick steel plates that were "made in a new manner," Dudley wrote Seward. "The metal is heated in pieces not more than a hundred pounds in weight and then rolled together. . . . They say the new mode is much more tenacious and its power of resistance much greater than the old. The order given is for fifteen hundred tons of plates."[2] By October, Dudley was reporting that the first ram would be completed by the middle of December. "They are using great precautions to keep us ignorant of their doings. No stranger is admitted into their yard. I shall send for my special detective at London and endeavor at the proper time to get up some evidence and have it laid before the government, but I have very little hope that they will do anything to stop them."[3]

Bitterly, Dudley went on to note that the Confederates were now constructing four ships for their navy in Liverpool and one more in Glasgow, and this "warranted Mr. Gladstone saying what he did at the New Castle dinner 'that the South was constructing a Navy.' If he had said England was constructing one for the South it would have been nearer the truth."

The energetic Liverpool spymaster continued to produce a steady stream of information on the activities of Confederate agents in Britain. He reported that at the end of January, one of his spies gained admittance to the Lairds' yard and talked with the workmen. They told the agent that the rams "are probably quite fast, that there are to be six watertight compartments and a compartment to run from fore to aft to let in water to sink her to a certain depth while in action. This is entirely new information." In the same dispatch, the consul informed the secretary of state that "a man of small stature with black whiskers under his chin without personal luggage came here in the steamer Europe this past day before yesterday. . . . He gave his name as Saunders or Sanders. He landed in a great hurry and started the same afternoon for London. He no doubt is a bearer of dispatches from the insurgents. May it not have been George Sanders?"[4] It turned out that Dudley was again correct. George Sanders was a principal Confederate agent in Europe.

Reporting on mass meetings of Northern sympathizers in Britain with members of the British Parliament present, Dudley commented that the gentlemen in charge "seem to be pushing matters vigorously" and that "the more meetings we can have the better public discussion must help us and damage the South." During this same period, Dudley reported to Adams that a ship named the *Georgiana,* built by the Confederates in Glasgow, was being loaded in Liverpool and would soon sail to augment the Confederate cruisers then in operation. Price Edwards, the collector of customs in Liverpool, once again denied that the ship was an armed naval vessel but suggested she was simply a blockade runner. As usual, the British government did nothing, and the *Georgiana* sailed on January 21. She ran aground while trying to slip past the Federal blockade at Charleston and was sunk by a Union gunboat. Benjamin Moran, referring to the incident in his journal, wrote: "The Collector of Customs at Liverpool connives openly and flagrantly at the preparation of these pirates. When proof is brought to him of the character of these ships he impudently meets it with a flat, unsupported denial and absolutely assists the corsairs to leave."[5]

On January 24, Dudley reported that a number of Frenchmen had arrived in Liverpool on their way to Charleston. "Fraser-Trenholm have agreed to pay their board at the hotel where they are stopping. From what I learn they are mechanics going to make army clothes." Dudley recommended in another report that the Federal forces give priority to the taking of Charleston, a major port receiving supplies from Britain, "I am satisfied that its capture would be regarded in this country as the death blow to the rebellion." He also reported on the activities of Confederate-sponsored clubs in Liverpool, gave the names of blockade runners and their sailing schedules, and provided drawings of the rams and the exact dimensions of the gunboat *Alexandra* being built in Scotland.

The painstaking research of the Quaker station chief is revealed in one of his reports to Seward on the *Alexandra*. On February 28, Dudley wrote Seward:

I understand that the Gun Boat building for the Southern Confederacy by Miller & Son is to be launched next week. The contract for building this steamer was made with Millers by Faucett Preston who are making the engines and all the armament. The contract is in their names but the money is paid by Fraser-Trenholm. This is the same arrangement they had with the building of the Oreto or Florida. I have been able to obtain the exact dimensions but have them from several different sources and they all agree within a few feet. The following may be relied on as very nearly her dimensions.

Length 145 feet over all. Moulded Beam 26 feet. Depth of hold 17 feet. Draught of water when loaded 9 to 10 feet. Her speed will be from 15 to 16 knots. Engines about 90 horsepower capable of being worked to some 200. She is built of wood very strong oak and teak with iron deck beams over engine and boilers, flat iron, sharp ends timbers caulked throughout. Her screw works in a copper slide weighing five tons and is so arranged as to be lifted out of the water. Her rig topsail schooner. Enclose marked No. 1, a drawing of this vessel as it is understood she will be when she is finished. I think the draftsman who made this is mistaken in his figures written on the plan. Enclosure No. 2 is a sketch of her Beam Shelf. I shall do what I can to stop her.[6]

Dudley informed the secretary of state at the end of March: "No expense is being spared" to make the ironclads "the most powerful and destructive vessels afloat. Nothing is being omitted that science and skill can suggest. The contractors have one of the largest yards in the kingdom and every facility and means for building vessels like these." Dudley ended his report with the warning: "You must not deceive yourselves, when finished they will have more power and speed probably than any Ironclad that have as yet been built."[7] Dudley's warnings prompted Congress and the American press to launch a vigorous national campaign to demand that the British government seize the Confederate ships or face war with the United States.

In the autumn of 1862, Minister Adams, responding to information Dudley had sent him on the construction of the new Rebel warships, wrote him: "Whenever you think you can get up as good evidence against them as you did in the case of No. 290 I should advise you to do it and send the papers to me as early as possible. Your proceedings in the Case of the No. 290 are a good guide. For you never did your country better service than by your labors on that occasion."[8]

Dudley immediately built up a case against the *Alexandra*. He used the information he already had that James Bulloch had made a contract for the warship and that Miller and Sons were building it through the agency of Fawcett, Preston and Company under orders from the manager of Fraser, Trenholm and Company. Once again, Dudley recruited the English lawyer A. F. Squarey, and the two men spent a number of months drawing up a legal case for the detention of the *Alexandra* under the Foreign Enlistment Act.

It was at this time that Dudley's espionage operation began to win serious support and recognition in Washington. The Northern public was seething over the piratical destruction of American merchant ships by the *Florida* and *Alabama*, while blockade runners from England continued to pour military supplies into Southern ports. Building of Confederate ironclad warships in English shipyards was seen to be intolerable by a public that now began to demand the creation of a Northern fleet of privateers to attack both blockade runners and the Rebel commerce raiders. Congress soon authorized the president to issue letters of marque as official support for privateers. On March 3, Lincoln signed the legislative action setting in motion the approval of Northern privateering. In London, Minister Adams became increasingly alarmed that such action would result in a war with Britain. During this anxious period, the U.S. Navy Department came up with a new idea to purchase Rebel warships under construction in Britain.

The idea had always been a favorite scheme of Freeman Morse, the American consul in London, and was now put forth by John Murray Forbes, a prominent business and political figure from Boston. After much argument among war leaders in Washington, including the consideration that Northern purchase of warships in England would place the North on the same moral plane as the South, thus undermining any claims against the depredations of the *Alabama,* the Navy Department decided to go ahead with the secret purchase scheme.

Forbes was called to New York by Secretary of the Treasury Salmon Chase. On March 15, 1863, Secretary of the Navy Welles, Chase, Forbes, and William Aspinwall, a New York businessman and shipowner, met together at the Fifth Avenue Hotel in New York City to discuss a project to buy Confederate warships under construction in England. This meeting set into motion what historians refer to as the Forbes-Aspinwall Mission. This mission was essentially a Washingon-sponsored covert operation. Only Thomas Dudley and Freeman Morse were informed of its purpose; Minister Adams was kept in the dark about the real goals of Forbes and Aspinwall.[9]

The two emissaries were to be provided with $10 million in new government bonds to be used as security for a loan of £1 million from the Baring Brothers in London. The money was to be used to purchase any warships built for the Rebel South. Forbes and Aspinwall were instructed to contact Dudley and Morse for advice in a campaign to undermine the Confederate shipbuilding program in Britain. Forbes sailed for Liverpool two days before the departure of Aspinwall and arrived in Liverpool on March 29, where he immediately went into conference with Dudley to dicuss the consul's effort to bring about the seizure of the Laird Rams.

Forbes, realizing that Dudley was not getting enough financial support from Washington for his espionage operations, advanced Dudley money to hire more detectives, promised that Aspinwall would provide more financial support, and wrote to Secretary of the Navy Welles that Dudley and his fellow consuls in Britain were found to be "in sad need of moral & effectual aid."[10] For the first time, Dudley and his network began to receive the official recognition they had so long deserved in their effective efforts against the Confederate naval program in Britain. Not wishing to involve Minister Adams in his covert operation, Forbes intimated to Adams that the purpose of his European mission was to recruit foreign soldiers for the Union army.

According to Douglas Maynard's monograph on the Forbes-Aspinwall Mission, Forbes had come to four important conclusions regarding Anglo-American relations: "First, letters of marque and reprisal should not be issued—it would only aid the enemy by causing trouble with England. Second, Admiral Charles Wilkes, commanding officer of the United States West India Squadron, was an obstacle to good relations between the two nations and should be removed: Everything he does hits twice as hard in irritating John Bull as the same thing done by anybody else." Third, "all the mercantile & upper classes" are "entirely against" the North, "but the emancipation movement is coming to our rescue, and the people are with us and are moving in their strength, and the vicious London *Times* shakes to hear them." Finally, Forbes thought that the course for the North to follow was to emphasize emancipation and to strike hard against the Confederates while "setting our teeth to avoid giving to the British ruling class any decided pretext for quarrelling with the North."[11]

In the autumn of 1862, the South arranged a multimillion dollar loan from a French banker named Erlanger, the loan being secured by cotton inventories. Forbes had also come to the conclusion that the successful floating of the $15 million Erlanger loan arranged by the South would remove its need to sell any of the ships already purchased or under construction. The ship-purchasing scheme was further undermined when, on April 7, the real purpose of the Forbes-Aspinwall Mission was exposed by an article in the London *Times,* which wrote that the two well-known merchants from the United States had arrived with sufficient U.S. bonds to buy up "the gunboats now building in England for the rebels." Forbes wrote to Gustavus Fox, assistant secretary of the navy: "I wish you could hang the man whoever he is who betrayed to the newspapers our plans here—it adds very much to our perplexities & to the difficulty of getting information."[12] Since the buyout scheme was intended to follow the South's pattern of purchasing vessels in the name of fictitious buyers, once secrecy was lost, the plan had to be abandoned.

The mission then turned its entire attention to building up Dudley's network. When Forbes was in London, he set up a system of coded telegrams to provide clandestine communication with Dudley. Forbes and Aspinwall together interceded with the State Department to increase its support for the spy network created by Dudley and Morse. They hoped to convince Seward that the Liverpool consul should devote his major efforts to the espionage operation targeted at the Confederate shipbuilding program. Dudley was further assured that Forbes and Aspinwall would provide additional funds for any counter-Confederate operation not supported by Adams. The two special envoys created two espionage zones in Britain, giving Dudley responsibility for the area north of the fifty-third parallel and Morse responsibility for port areas lying to the south.[13] Forbes then devoted all his energy to the propaganda campaign against the Confederacy, calling upon editors of English newspapers, reprinting pro-Northern editorials, and making a careful analysis of British public opinion in relation to the war.

William Evarts, an eminent attorney and friend of Seward's, subsequently arrived in Liverpool to assist Forbes, Aspinwall, and Dudley in their effort to utilize British law to detain Confederate warships. In particular, Evarts worked closely with Dudley to prepare the case against the *Alexandra*. At the height of all this American activity to thwart the construction of a Rebel navy, the British Parliament opened a heated debate on the question of the Foreign Enlistment Act. American senator Charles Sumner had written a series of letters to Richard Cobden warning him of the dangerous temper of Northern opinion over the depredations of the *Florida* and *Alabama* and the prospects for the commission of privateers to stop them. Sumner pleaded with Cobden to move against the new Southern rams under construction: "Stop them pray. Stop them." As a result of this plea, Cobden wrote Russell arguing that "something more than mere passiveness was due to a friendly government," and that "our authorities ought to exercise greater vigilance in enforcing the observance of our own law."[14]

On March 27, pro-Northern members of Parliment, led by William Forster, Richard Cobden, and John Bright, opened the debate on the Foreign Enlistment Act. Forster blamed the government for allowing the *Alabama* to escape and demanded that the Palmerston cabinet do everything in its power to maintain neutrality in the war. Others argued that there had been no unreasonable delay in acting upon the evidence supplied by Ambassador Adams in the case of the *Alabama*. Laird, who was building ships for the Confederates, informed Parliament that at the beginning of the war, his firm had been approached to build ships for the U.S. Federal government. Replying to Bright, Laird argued that the North had purchased large quantities of weapons from England, whereas the South had received only "two ships, unarmed and unfit for any purpose of warfare, for they procured their armaments somewhere else." When it was his turn to speak, Palmerston counterattacked the claims of Forster and Bright, whom he referred to as "the mouthpieces of the North." The prime minister adamantly refused to amend the Foreign Enlistment Act at the behest of one of the belligerents.[15]

Once again the American community in Britain was depressed by the intransigence and biased neutrality of the Palmerston regime. On the other hand, the tide of British opinion in opposition to slavery had began to rise under a skillful campaign of the Emancipation Society, led by John Stuart Mill, Edward Dicey, Harriet Martineau, and John Cairnes, who had countered Spence's defense of the South with his own book, *Slave Power*. The Emancipation Society organized highly successful public meetings to stop the building of warships for the Southern slaveholders.

Dudley's detective, Matthew Maguire, reported to the counsel at the end of March on the launching of the *Alexandra*. His spies revealed that representatives from Fraser, Trenholm and Company, Captain Bulloch, Captain Butcher, who had commanded the *Alabama* when she escaped, and some ladies were all present at the launching. Maguire informed Dudley that he had been in communication with men working on the ship and had been told by them that she was a gunboat "built for the Confederates or Southerners as some called them."

On March 28, while Parliament was debating British neutrality, Dudley presented his evidence to the collector of customs, requesting that the *Alexandra* be detained on the grounds that the ship was a Confederate cruiser in violation of the Foreign Enlistment Act. Two days later, Ambassador Adams sent all of Dudley's evidence on the *Alexandra* to the Foreign Office, telling Lord Russell that the vessel was in violation of England's neutrality. Lord Russell, following the precedent of the *Alabama* affair, sent the documents to the lords of the Treasury and law officers for an opinion. The lords of the Treasury argued that the *Alexandra* was simply a strongly built merchant ship, but the law officers were convinced by Dudley's evidence that the vessel was, in fact, a warship, constituting a violation of the Foreign Enlistment Act.[16]

In an unprecedented action, Lord Russell followed the advice of the law officers and ordered that the ship be detained. Custom officials seized the *Alexandra* on April 5, 1863, just as the ship was fitting out to go to sea. Dudley and Adams, through their persistence, had won a historic victory. Adams wrote Seward that he now felt that the "government is really disposed to maintain its neutrality." He continued, "I rejoice at this symptom of a disposition to defeat the mechanizations of those who hope to relieve the rebels."[17] Seward was naturally elated over the detention of the *Alexandra* and wrote to Dudley: "I am directed to assure you of the high appreciation which is entertained by the President of the well directed energy and discreet proceedings by means of which you have successfully accomplished this important object."[18]

A number of circumstances combined to influence Lord Russell's decision to take action against the construction of Confederate warships in British yards. Perhaps a major cause of the foreign minister's change of heart was a European crisis involving France and Russia over events in Poland. As the historian Brian Jenkins notes, "If England was to exercise a restraining influence upon the French emperor a quiescent relationship with the United States was essential." Lord Russell "continued to fret about the possibility of the European and American crises becoming entangled."[19]

Months earlier, Russell had expressed concern over "the spectacle of the *Alabama* cruising the oceans 'with English guns and English sailors to burn, sink and destroy' the ships of a friendly nation."[20] The British foreign minister had even given some thought to the future prospect of indemnities demanded by the United States from Britain for American ships destroyed by Confederate gunboats built in British shipyards. Moreover, the precedents established by Confederate privateers could well face Britain in any future war. In any case, the growing anger of the Northern public in the United States and the mass movement against Confederate agents in Britain put added pressure on Russell to uphold British neutrality. Russell was ready to allow the law courts to take over the task of enforcing the Foreign Enlistment Act.

In the coming year, Consul Dudley would confront Russell with some of his own arguments. On January 11, 1864, Dudley sent a letter to Russell containing three affidavits making the case that the *Alabama* was, in fact, a British ship. Dudley verified the fact that families of British seamen serving on the *Alabama* "were paid once a month here in Liverpool by Mr. G. Klingender and Fraser Trenholm & Co. the one half part of the wages earned by the men on board this vessel." Affidavits by John Latham, his wife, and another seaman serving on the *Alabama* testified to the fact that their families received wages monthly in Liverpool.

Dudley summed up his case by stating, "I regard these affidavits as important for the character of nationality (if she has any) of this vessel which was built in England; fitted out in England; armed with English guns and manned by English seamen; supplied with coal and other necessaries while cruising from England in English vessels by English merchants; and the wages earned by the men while serving on board paid here—all stamp her, as it seems to me, if anything can, as an English piratical craft."[21]

As a lawyer and head of Union intelligence operations in England, Dudley was laying the basis for the U.S. case against England in the postwar period. The evidence amassed by Dudley would be presented before an international tribunal meeting in Switzerland in 1871, which would award the United States substantial indemnity payments by Britain for the depredations of the *Alabama*.

Shortly after the *Alexandra* seizure, Forbes assigned Dudley to tour the major northern ports in search of all ships under construction for the Rebel navy. Dudley reported to Seward on May 2: "On Monday morning last I left home to go through the districts lying North of Hull & Liverpool to inaugurate a system to prevent any more privateers or war vessels leaving England without our knowledge; and to adopt some plan to obtain evidence sufficient to stop the Ironclad ram building by George & James Thompson at Glasgow for the Insurgents."[22]

When the *Alexandra* trial opened at the end of June, Dudley and Adams were once again confronted with the convolutions of the British legal system. Tories and Confederate sympathizers forced a new debate in Parliament on the seizure of the *Alexandra,* while the defendants in the case retained brilliant counsel to oppose the inexperienced solicitor general for the Crown. The shipbuilders' defense team made an all-out effort to discredit Dudley's main witness, Clarence Yonge, the former paymaster on the *Alabama,* by claiming that he had deserted his wife and child in Savannah, then married a well-to-do mulatto woman in Kingston, Jamaica, whom he also abandoned after getting hold of her money.

The elderly judge in the trial, Jonathon Frederick Pollock, turned out to be a Confederate sympathizer. He instructed the jury that the Foreign Enlistment Act was intended only to stop armed vessels, and that there was nothing unlawful about the escape of the *Alabama.* The jury's verdict of "not guilty" for William Miller and Sons, builders of the *Alexandra,* was thus a foregone conclusion. The law officers immediately appealed the verdict, the *Alexandra* detention continuing until a decision came down from the higher courts.[23]

Both Dudley and Adams were disgusted by the incompetence displayed by the Crown in prosecuting its case. Dudley, as a lawyer, wrote Seward that he had never seen a case so poorly tried. Edmond Hammond, the permanent undersecretary at the Foreign Office, commented privately that if Judge Pollock's opinion prevailed, the Foreign Enlistment Act was simply "a cheat and a delusion." As a result of the *Alexandra* decision, Secretary of State Seward instructed Adams to inform Russell that the United States might send Union warships into neutral ports to intercept privateers.[24] Tension between the two countries rose to new heights.

Thomas Dudley never forgave the British for failing to enforce their own neutrality laws. As a result of the *Alexandra* trial, a number of detectives working for Dudley quit because they believed that they would not be employed after the war. Neil Black, an important witness for the Crown in the *Alexandra* case, was blacklisted from British shipyards for his cooperation with Dudley. Other shipyard workers who presented evidence for the Crown were also fired. A few years before his death, Dudley bitterly recalled the refusal of Lord Russell to accept the testimony of Clarence Yonge as credible evidence. Dudley's retrospective comments on his long legal struggle to prevent the construction of Confederate warships in Britain reveal the obstacles he confronted:

> [Lord Russell] used this term "credible evidence" because among the affidavits that had been sent to the English government there was one made by Clarence Randolph Yonge, who had been purser on board the steamer *Alabama,* and who was conversant with all the doings of the Confederate government in Europe with regard to the construction of war vessels. He had left the *Alabama* and was in Liverpool.

He knew what everybody in Liverpool knew, except the officers of her majesty's government, that these vessels were being built for the Confederates. I obtained Yonge's affidavit, proving the fact they were being built for the rebels. With this affidavit the proof was complete. It brought home the construction directly for the Confederate government, and hence the necessity of either ignoring the affidavit or stopping the vessels from sailing. Earl Russell took it upon himself to ignore the affidavit. He threw it out on the ground that it was not credible. He did this in a preliminary proceeding, contrary to all practice and all precedent under English law as practiced in England or the United States. The difficulty about Mr. Yonge, to whom Earl Russell objected, was this: On one of the voyages of the *Alabama* to the West Indies, Yonge, while purser, had married a quadroon girl, a native of the West Indies. It was this act of marrying a quadroon girl that had tainted him in the estimation of Earl Russell, and justified the rejection of the evidence on the ground that it was not credible. His affidavit was not even to be considered, much less regarded. To this extent was the English government driven to shield the Confederates and enable them to get their war-vessels out.[25]

The Quaker consul well understood the prevalence of racism among the British upper classes in Victorian England.

Forbes and Aspinwall left England for home on June 30. After returning to Washington, Forbes wrote Seward requesting that more funds be set aside for Dudley to pursue his case against the rams. In London, the news of the stunning twin victories by Union armies at Gettysburg and Vicksburg appeared finally to doom Confederate hopes for recognition. Henry Adams wrote to his father: "The disasters of the rebels are unredeemed by even any hope for success. It is now conceded that all idea of intervention is at an end." The impending completion of the Laird Rams, however, would once again bring Britain and the United States to the brink of war.

The historian Brian Jenkins notes that in June, Cobden visited Russell and "informed him with all the emphasis he could muster, and with the authority of a man who claimed 'considerable knowledge' of the United States, the foreign secretary's American policy was leading 'either to a war or great humiliation.' The warning was repeated publicly by the radical press. American exasperation at the immense damage inflicted on their commerce by British-built raiders would surely boil over if the rams were permitted to get out, for they seemed capable of breaking the blockade."[26] A number of British leaders were becoming aware of the precedents established by a narrow reading of the Foreign Enlistment Act, which in the future would allow British enemies to build warships in American ports. A noisy campaign in the British press was subsequently launched to stop the rams.

James Bulloch now faced a difficult task in getting his rams out of Britain. His efforts were plagued by Dudley's spy network, parliamentary inquiries, protests led by the Emancipation Society, and letters to the newspapers. Bulloch was careful not to be seen in the vicinity of the Laird shipyard and cleverly transferred ownership of the two rams under construction to the French firm of Messrs. Bravay and Company. Bravay claimed that he had been commissioned by the viceroy of Egypt to purchase the ironclads.

Dudley was not deceived by Bulloch's standard ruse of disguising his warships under foreign ownership. The Liverpool consul had been collecting information on the rams for more than a year. On July 3, his agents reported that the British steamer *Gibraltar* would carry the guns for the new warships, and that the first ram would be launched on July 4.

Forbes had been very impressed by one of Dudley's spies, a young man by the name of George Chapman who worked in the Lairds' yards. Forbes turned over money to Dudley to pay Chapman for the extensive reports he submitted on the rams. On July 7, Dudley made a formal application to the collector of customs to detain what he considered to be the "most formidable and dangerous ships afloat." He supported this request with a number of affidavits.[27]

William Russell and Joseph Ellis, master shipwrights, testified that they had made an inspection of the first ram before it was launched and described it as "an iron-clad vessel-of-war" armed with a projecting ram designed to sink other vessels. They stated: "We have no hesitation in saying that the said vessel is an iron-clad Ram of the most formidable description, and cannot be intended for any purpose but that of war." Dudley submitted two more affidavits, one by Clarence Yonge and the other by George Chapman, testifying that the warships were constructed by James Bulloch through the agency Fraser, Trenholm and Company. Dudley personally carried copies of the affidavits to London and turned them over to Adams.

The American minister realized a crisis was at hand. Writing in his diary, he noted that the matter of the rams was "the gravest event of the series" and must be handled "with corresponding seriousness." Dudley informed Adams that the authorities in Liverpool accepted the Lairds' statement that the rams were ordered by Egypt or Turkey. Palmerston confirmed this report at the end of July when replying to Cobden's question about the rams, stating that the ships were intended for the French.

Also at the end of July, Dudley informed Adams that he had learned from the French consul in Liverpool that the new warships were not constructed for the French government. During this period, Dudley traveled up to Glasgow to take a look at the ram under construction there. The consul appeared to enjoy his work. He wrote Seward: "On Thursday of last week I went to Glasgow and took with me one of my men. I obtained a good view of the Ram building for the Confederates by George Thompson from the river which is very narrow. She is up high and so much exposed that I could see her as if in the yard. Only a part of the armour plates are on as yet, and from appearances I should judge she could not be ready for launching for two months at least."[28] Informants told him the new gunboat would be called the *Virginia.* Dudley also informed Seward that the British press was reporting the intention of the Federal navy to commence firing on any ship that attempted to run the blockade of Southern ports. The consul remarked that whether or not the report was true, the threat was undermining the Confederate effort to recruit seamen in Britain to run the blockade.

By the end of August, work on the Liverpool rams rushed to completion. The turrets on the first ram were mounted on the twenty-eighth, and the second was launched on the twenty-ninth. Both Adams and Russell were on vacation in Scotland, but Russell wrote Adams on September 1 that Dudley's evidence was simply hearsay, Confederate ownership had not been proven, and the English government therefore found no grounds for detention. All through the summer months, Russell answered all questions from inside and outside the government concerning the rams with the same insistence that nothing could be done without evidence, Dudley's research was "in great measure hearsay," and that there was no legal evidence contradicting ownership of the rams by Bravay.

Adams returned from his vacation in Scotland on September 3 to find awaiting him Russell's note refusing to detain the rams. In an immediate reply to Russell, Adams warned of "the grave nature of the situation in which both countries must be placed in the event of an act of aggression committed against the government and people of the United States by either of these formidable vessels." The minister received information from Dudley the next day that one of the rams had successfully completed its trial run and was ready for sea. Adams then sent off two more notes to Russell. The last one, dated September 5, 1863, quoted the Confederate boasts that the new ironclads would be used to invade the harbors of New York, Boston, and Portland and break the Federal blockade against the South. Adams concluded the note with his famous declaration warning Russell of the consequences of the escape of the Confederate rams: "It would be superfluous in me to point out to your lordship that this is war."[29] Dudley went up to London to wait out the crisis with the minister.

Dudley recalls:

Mr. Adams [was] in a very depressed state of mind; he regarded war
with England as inevitable. I shall never forget how he walked up and
down his drawing room, discussing the gravity of the situation. He
said, "We would have only nineteen days more in England; that he
would have to leave as soon as he heard from Washington . . . but he
could see no alternative but war. The Rebellion had been kept alive
by the aid and assistance it had received from England. There were
hundreds of English steamers and vessels then engaged in carrying
munitions of war and supplies from England for the rebel army,
besides the war-vessels which had been built and were then in the
course of construction in the kingdom. They had their financial
department, their commissary department, their ordnance department, and their naval department in England; and it had come
almost to this, that the war was actually being conducted and carried
on against us by Englishmen, and from England. The matter had
been fully considered by our government, and it was prepared to take
action. It could not permit matters to go further than they had gone.
Our government could not do otherwise than it had done, and there
was no way out of it but war. The English navy was superior to ours,
and it was quite likely that they would defeat us on the ocean, and
might inflict much damage, perhaps burn some of the cities on the
sea-coast; but we would have the advantage on the land, and could
march our forces into Canada and capture those provinces; but no
one could compute the consequences,—the human lives that would
be taken, or the damages that would be done, or the treasure that
would be spent in the prosecution of such a war."

This was a remarkable recapitulation of the distress experienced by the
small community of American diplomats in Britain during the Civil War.

Dudley states that it was fortunate that the people at home "did not
know the perilous condition of affairs in England. . . . They had enough at
home to bear in the conduct of the war without having this added." Then
Dudley recalls that while he and Adams were pacing up and down in the
minister's drawing-room, he "observed through a side window a Queen's
messenger approaching the house. The bell rang, and soon Mr. Adams's ser-
vant delivered to him a despatch which the messenger had brought. He
opened it and read it aloud." The note was from Lord Russell stating that Her
Majesty's government still had the detention of the Laird Rams under consid-

eration. Dudley said to Adams that the English government was backing down, and Adams replied that it looked that way.[30]

The diplomatic archives reveal that Russell had already determined to detain the rams on September 3, but had not taken the courtesy of informing Adams of his decision. Russell acted on his own initiative because Palmerston was on a trip to Wales. When Palmerston returned, however, he approved of the decision by his foreign minister. It was only on September 8 that Adams and Dudley learned the rams had been detained. The crisis was coming to a close. World public opinion and the strength of Northern armies combined to discourage the idea of foreign intervention in America's war.

Once back in Liverpool, however, Dudley reported that work on the rams was continuing at breakneck speed. On September 11, Adams received a note from the American consul in Cardiff stating that a number of seamen had come off a French brig that had transported them from Brest, where the raider *Florida* had put up for repairs. These men claimed to be the crew for the rams and soon boarded a train for Liverpool. The consul raised the key question in their regard: Why would Confederate crewmen be dispatched if the rams were not preparing to leave?

Dudley, who kept a close watch on the Laird yard, reported to Adams that one of the ironclads was in the final stage of completion. He could see nothing to prevent the warship from sailing and doubted whether the authorities had ever formally informed the Lairds that the rams were to be detained.

On September 10, Sen. Charles Sumner delivered a major speech in New York attacking Britain for its unfriendly policy toward the American government. Sumner called on the Palmerston government to reconsider its course and thus prevent a war between Britain and the United States. Lord Russell made a public reply to Sumner's attack on September 26, stating that Britain would never yield to threats. He then went on to publicly defend his decision to detain the Confederate rams as part of a larger government design to preserve British neutrality in the American Civil War. Russell's speech won widespread public approval in England. He had rebuked Sumner while at the same time proving that Britain was truly neutral in the American conflict.[31] In retrospect, it is clear that the threat of war by Adams, Dudley, and the American Congress should the rams escape forced the hand of the Palmerston government.

Unknown to Adams and Dudley was the continuing debate in the British cabinet on the question of how the rams might be legally detained. During September, Russell and Palmerston came up with a definitive solution to the whole problem. The British government could resolve the crisis by purchasing the warships from the Frenchman Bravay, who claimed legal ownership.

Finally, on October 8, as one of the rams was preparing to sail, Russell ordered the seizure of both warships. The law officers of the Crown supported Russell's action two weeks later. All work on the vessels was subsequently stopped; the warships were put under guard until the government purchased the ships in the spring of 1864. Dudley and Adams had, in effect, stopped the building of a modern Confederate navy in Great Britain.

On hearing of the detention of the rams, William Evarts, the prominent New York lawyer sent to England by Seward to assist the Liverpool consul in legal proceedings, wrote to Dudley, "You have had the greatest share of labor, solicitude and responsibility in this business, and are entitled to the principal credit and congratulations for the invaluable result." The State Department also sent congratulations, and William Whiting, solicitor of the War Department, who had recently returned from England, wrote Dudley: "It is difficult here to make our people appreciate the difficulty and importance of your labors. They who are rescued from danger are too apt to disbelieve in danger."[32] Dudley and Adams had sunk the Confederate navy before it had put to sea.

CHAPTER 8

Final Days of the
Florida and *Alabama*

WHILE THOMAS HAINES DUDLEY AND CHARLES FRANCIS ADAMS CARRIED ON their fight against the Confederate rams, the *Florida* and *Alabama* continued to sweep the seas of U.S. merchant ships. The historian James McPherson concludes that although the Rebel cruisers "did not alter the outcome of the war, they diverted numerous Union navy ships from the blockade, drove insurance rates for American vessels to astronomical heights, forced these vessels to remain in port or convert to foreign registry, and helped topple the American merchant marine from its once dominant position, which it never regained."[1]

The most famous offspring of the *Florida* was the captured brig *Clarence*. Commander Maffitt placed his most able young officer, Lt. Charles Read, in command. Read made a daring cruise along the East Coast, where, after transferring his guns from one ship to another, he burned his previous raider and thus, according to Stern, "baffled the Federal Navy, which sought him in vain while he took prize after prize only a few miles offshore."[2] In late June 1863, Read sailed into Portland Harbor, Maine, in one of the most audacious raids of the war, to capture the revenue cutter *Caleb Cushing*, which was lying alongside a wharf. In the ensuing battle, Read and his Confederate officers were captured and then imprisoned at Fort Warren in Boston Harbor. Read was exchanged in October and at the end of the war commanded a Confederate ram on the Mississippi.

Captain Maffitt ended his command of the *Florida* on August 23, 1863, when, in poor health, he turned the Confederate raider over to Commodore J. N. Barney at Brest Harbor in France. However, Barney's health also failed before he could put to sea, and he was replaced by C. M. Morris on January 5, 1864. The new commander sailed to Madeira in early February and, on the way to the West Indies, captured and burned a Yankee ship, the *Avon*, from Boston. After arriving in Bermuda, the *Florida* remained in the British port until the end of June.

While at anchor in Bermuda, Morris received a letter of instruction from Confederate Secretary of the Navy Stephen Russell Mallory, authorizing him to receive $50,000 from Bulloch to finance his current cruise. Mallory then suggested "a dash at New England commerce." Morris set sail for the New England coast, making several captures on the way. On July 10, the *Florida* captured four ships in one day.

Through fear of the Northern navy or for other reasons, Morris abandoned the New England cruise and crossed the Atlantic to the Canary Islands, where he recoaled and then headed for the Brazilian coast. The *Florida* made its last capture on September 26, 1864, and on October 4 entered the Brazilian port of Bahia. There the cruise of the *Florida* came to an inglorious end when the ambitious Capt. Napoleon Collins of the U.S. warship *Wachusett* captured the Confederate ship as it lay at anchor while most of its crew was ashore. In the middle of the night, the *Wachusett* sideswiped the *Florida*, carrying away its mizzenmast and crushing its bulwarks. After small-arms fire broke out between the two ships, the *Wachusett* backed off and fired cannon shots into the Confederate raider. Deciding that it was impossible to put up a fight, the lieutenant commanding the *Florida* surrendered.[3]

Collins put a prize crew aboard the Rebel cruiser and then towed the ship all the way to Hampton Roads, Virginia, a port held by the U.S. Navy. Since the Federal warship had violated the international rights of neutral Brazil, the U.S. government found it necessary to apologize to Brazil. But despite his violation of international law, Captain Collins, like Captain Wilkes of the *Trent* affair, was treated as a national hero. Some months later, the *Florida*, with her twin smokestacks and rakish masts, was mysteriously sunk while under Federal supervision at Newport News. Altogether in her brief career, the *Florida* destroyed thirty-eight American ships.

All through the winter of 1863, Semmes and the *Alabama* burned or captured Northern ships off the coast of Jamaica and then Brazil. A cartoon from *Harper's Weekly* titled "The PIRATE ALABAMA" recorded the fact that most of the property destroyed by the "pirate Semmes" was insured in England, and the losses would consequently be borne by Englishmen.

Subsequently, Semmes set sail for South Africa; seized the Northern bark *Sea Bride* just offshore from Cape Town, where huge crowds gathered to watch its capture; and then anchored in the bay. Vistors in small boats, including photographers and the press, came aboard to inspect the famous Confederate raider. On August 14, Semmes learned of Lee's defeat at Gettysburg. Subsequently, after a month's cruise in the South Atlantic, the Confederate commander returned to Cape Town, where he was informed of the loss of Vicksburg. He was becoming discouraged and noted in his diary, "How tiresome is the routine of cruising becoming."[4]

Aware that the Federal warship *Vanderbilt* was in the area searching for the *Alabama,* Semmes set sail for the Far East. After a three-thousand-mile voyage, the *Alabama* announced its presence by sinking and burning a number of American merchant ships in the area. At the same time, Gideon Welles, secretary of the U.S. Navy, sent the Federal warship *Wyoming* to the Far East to find and destroy the *Alabama.*

On arriving at the Sunda Strait, between Sumatra and Java, Semmes discovered that the USS *Wyoming* was hunting for him in those waters. Although determined to fight the Federal warship, he never found her. On December 21, the *Alabama* sailed into the harbor of Singapore where Semmes found dozens of American ships anchored. Thomas Dudley learned many years later from Henry William Alcott, former sailmaker on the *Alabama,* that Semmes had been forced to escape from Singapore after only three days in port because some five hundred crewmen from American ships had armed themselves, commandeered a number of small boats, and were preparing to capture the *Alabama* as it lay at anchor.[5]

During the final days of 1863, the *Alabama* captured a number of ships in the Strait of Malacca before beginning its long voyage back to the Atlantic. Having put his prisoners ashore in India, Semmes arrived in Cape Town after a cruise of six months. There, reading American papers, he learned that the South was losing the war. He recalls in his memoirs: "Our people were being harder and harder pressed." The loss of Vicksburg and the battle of Gettysburg had weakened the South, the blockade of Southern ports was tightening, and "our finances were rapidly deteriorating and a general demoralization, in consequence, seemed to be spreading among our people. From the whole review of 'the situation,' I was very apprehensive that the cruises of the *Alabama* were drawing to a close."[6]

Heading up from the Cape of Good Hope to the equatorial crossing, the *Alabama* captured a number of Yankee ships homeward bound from the Pacific. On May 2, the raider crossed the equator into the Northern Hemisphere. Semmes was forced to admit that the "poor old *Alabama* was not now what she had been" in the past.

She was like the wearied fox-hound, limping back after a long chase, foot sore, and longing for quiet and repose. Her commander, like herself, was well-nigh worn out. Vigils by night and day, the storm and drenching rain, the frequent and rapid change of climate, now freezing, now melting or broiling, and the constant excitement of the chase and capture, had laid, in the three years of war he had been afloat, a load of a dozen years on his shoulders. The shadows of a sorrowful future, too, began to rest upon his spirit. The last batch of newspapers captured were full of disasters. Might it not be, that after all our trials, the cause for which we were struggling would be lost?[7]

In the winter of 1864, the *Florida* and the *Alabama* were the only Confederate commerce raiders at sea. The *Alabama* now found few ships to sink, because most American merchant vessels had transferred to foreign flags. But on April 23, the *Alabama* captured the *Rockingham,* a ship carrying fertilizer. Semmes took off his usual supply of stores plus the ship's chronometer, removed the crew, and then used the *Rockingham* as target practice for his own gun crews. He discovered during this shelling that his gunpowder had deteriorated, every third shell failing to explode. Nevertheless, five days later, he captured and burned a Yankee merchant ship, the *Tycoon.* This was the last ship destroyed by the *Alabama.* Needing repairs, the ship headed north for the coast of France. On June 10, she reached the English Channel, where the next day a French pilot took the battered ship into the harbor at Cherbourg.

Historian Stern records that while Semmes was in Cherbourg:

The *Times* printed a long letter he had written at sea. In it he said that the British Queen's Proclamation of Neutrality, which had inspired other nations to take a similar stand, had made it necessary for him to destroy Yankee shipping because it prohibited him from taking captured prizes into a port where they could be sold and put to use. England could still revoke "her unjust and unnatural orders," he suggested. But all his letter accomplished was to make the United States Government more eager than ever to collect damages from Britain for the destruction done by Confederate raiders she had built.[8]

Thomas Dudley continued to devote a great deal of time to the taking of depositions from masters and crewmen attached to vessels sunk by the *Alabama* and other Confederate cruisers. The Liverpool consul shouldered the main responsibility for compiling the record that would be the basis for the *Alabama* claims submitted by the U.S. government to an international tribunal after the war. As Stern notes, "The British had long been hostile to the idea of paying anything for the damage done by the Confederate cruisers built in their shipyards. The war had been profitable, for it had practically eliminated the United States as their most important rival in carrying the ocean traffic of the world. Semmes and his fellow captains had done their work so well by destroying 110,000 tons of commercial shipping that most American vessels had been driven off the high seas."[9]

William Dayton, the U.S. minister to France, learning of the *Alabama's* presence in Cherbourg Harbor, sent a telegram to Capt. John Winslow, commander of the USS *Kearsarge,* which was anchored nearby at Flushing. The *Kearsarge* soon was cruising outside the Cherbourg Harbor, and Semmes, determined to fight her, sent a challenge to Winslow stating: "My intention is to fight the Kearsarge as soon as I can make the necessary arrangements. . . . I beg she will not depart before I am ready to go out."[10]

The historical record reveals that Semmes and Winslow had been roommates on a warship in the old navy and had fought together in the Mexican War. According to Stern: "They were exact opposites in character. Winslow, although Southern born, had been educated in New England and had married a Boston girl. He had become an ardent abolitionist who felt that it was his duty to help exterminate slavery and subjugate the South."[11]

On Sunday, June 19, at ten o'clock in the morning, some fifteen thousand people gathered to watch the spectacle of an American Civil War sea battle in European waters. Among the spectators was the son of Minister William Dayton, who would give a full account of the battle to Thomas Dudley. A more renowned observer was Edouard Manet, the Impressionist painter, who had come down with other sightseers on a special train from Paris. Manet went out on a French fishing boat to paint the battle at close range. His painting of the historic sea battle is now in the John S. Johnson Collection in Philadelphia.

Dayton's son, who had stationed himself on high ground with a telescope, recorded that around "nine o'clock the English yacht *Deerhound . . .* ran out a little towards the breakwater. After apparently observing for a few minutes, she returned and went alongside the *Alabama.* She then stood out again straight through the Western pass to sea; about two miles out she headed more to the *Kearsarge.* The *Alabama* then came out by the same pass and stood straight out to sea, the yacht running up and apparently communicating with her."[12] The mysterious role of the *Deerhound* would once again bring London and Washington into bitter conflict.

Owned by John Lancaster, a Confederate sympathizer, the trim British yacht had been built in the Laird shipyards and was, in fact, a smaller version of the *Alabama.* After the battle, as controversy erupted over the relationship between the two ships during the engagement, Lancaster denied that he had ever been in communication with the *Alabama,* and claimed that he was simply following the request of his children, who wished to see the battle.

The *Alabama* and *Kearsarge* were evenly matched, the former carrying six thirty-two-pound guns, one sixty-eight-pounder, and one hundred-pound pivot rifled cannon, while the latter had four thirty-two-pounders, one twenty-eight-pounder rifle, and two formidable eleven-inch Dahlgren shell guns mounted on pivots fore and aft. Both ships measured about two hundred feet in length and carried two steam engines, although the engines of the *Kearsarge* could produce four hundred horsepower to three hundred for the *Alabama.* The *Kearsarge* carried a crew of 163 men, the *Alabama* 149.

Stern observes:

> The odds of battle favored the Federal ship. The Alabama was travel worn, her foul bottom slowed her down, and her gunpowder was stale. Most important of all, the middle section of the Kearsarge where the engines were, was protected by heavy iron chains draped along her sides and fastened to the planking—a method of defense which had originated on the Mississippi River. And since the chains had been neatly boxed over with boards painted the same color as the rest of the hull, Semmes later claimed he did not know he was about to go into combat with a ship that was partially armored.[13]

Semmes's claim of ignorance regarding the use of chains to protect the hull of the *Kearsarge* was later put in doubt by his own lieutenant, Arthur Sinclair, who claimed that Semmes already knew about the chain armor utilized by Winslow.[14]

It was a clear, sunny day with a calm sea when the two ships converged for battle, one heading east, the other west, then circling in narrowing spirals, each facing the other with starboard broadsides. The *Alabama* fired first from a distance of a mile. One shell from her hundred-pound gun lodged in the wooden steering post of the *Kearsarge,* but because of a defective fuse, it did not explode; another sheared off the top mast of the engine room hatch. One sixty-eight-pound shell from the *Alabama*'s Blakely gun exploded among the gun crew of the after pivot gun, wounding three men, one of whom later died.

Accurate countershelling from the *Kearsarge* then began to smash into the *Alabama.* Shells from the two eleven-inch Dahlgrens disabled the after pivot gun of the Confederate raider, bulwarks were torn away, shells began to explode between decks and in the engine room. Lieutenant Sinclair records that when one of the *Alabama*'s guns had been loaded and run out to fire, "an

11-inch shell struck full in the middle of the first man on the port side of the gun, passing through the entire lot, killing or wounding them, and piling up on the deck a mass of human fragments."[15] Semmes, himself wounded in the right arm, then had some sail rigged and attempted to steer the ship to the French coast. When he determined this was not possible, he struck his colors and sent a dinghy to the *Kearsarge* to arrange a surrender.

In a battle lasting little more than an hour, the *Alabama* was now sinking rapidly. Responding to the disaster around him, Semmes hurled his sword into the sea. Since most of his boats were smashed, he ordered all hands to save themselves and plunged overboard himself. Winslow then hailed the British yacht *Deerhound* and shouted: "For God's sake, do what you can to save them!" The British steamer immediately set off for the sinking *Alabama*. A boat from the *Deerhound* pulled in Semmes and his chief officer, Kell, among others. Kell hid Semmes in the bottom of the boat, and when a launch from the *Kearsarge* pulled alongside looking for Semmes, Kell told the Union sailors that Semmes had drowned. Two remaining boats from the *Alabama* carried seventy crewmen to the *Kearsarge,* where they were taken prisoner. Some thirty men on the *Alabama* were either killed by gunfire or drowned.[16]

Once the survivors were aboard the *Deerhound,* the British ship steamed directly for the British port of Southampton, and once there, all the Confederates were put ashore. When one of the officers on the *Kearsarge* told Winslow that Semmes was probably aboard the *Deerhound* and that the British ship appeared to be escaping with its Confederate survivors, Winslow replied, "No Englishman who flies the royal yacht flag would act so dishonorable a part as to run away with his prisoners when he had been asked to save them from drowning."[17] By this time, the *Deerhound* was too far off on its way to England to be caught.

Captain Winslow, Charles Francis Adams, and Thomas Dudley were naturally incensed at Lancaster, the owner of the *Deerhound,* for refusing to hand over Semmes and the other Confederate sailors as prisoners of war. The strain between Washington and London was further increased when Semmes was lionized by the British press and treated as a hero in London. When Adams wrote a letter of protest to Lord Russell, the British foreign minister replied: "It appears to me that the owner of the *Deerhound* performed only a common duty of humanity in saving from the waves the captain and several of the crew of the *Alabama*. They would otherwise, in all probability, have been drowned, and thus would never have been in the situation of prisoners of war. It does not appear to me to be any part of the duty of a neutral to assist in making prisoners of war for one of the belligerents."[18]

Russell ignored the fact that the *Alabama* never would have existed if it had not been built in British shipyards in violation of Britain's own Foreign Enlistment Act. Stern reveals British motivation for their action: "The fact that the *Alabama* was a British-built vessel which had never touched Confederate soil and which was operated by a crew that was largely British undoubtedly had something to do with the great enthusiasm shown in England for Semmes and his men."[19]

Margaret Dayton, wife of the U.S. minister to France, wrote to Dudley, giving him details of the destruction of the *Alabama* as witnessed by her son Willie. She commented, "What a pity Semmes could not have gone down with her, but your English had to help him off." Five days after the battle, Captain Winslow wrote to Dudley, "The *Deerhound* ran off with the prisoners, which I did not believe any cur dog could have been guilty of under the circumstances."[20]

Official British sympathy for the Southern slavepower throughout the Civil War accounts for the frequent bitterness displayed by both Dudley and Adams toward England. Both did whatever they could to undermine Semmes's London reputation in an attempt to counteract the public acclaim for "the daring world cruise of the valiant *Alabama*" promulgated in the press.

A pamphlet soon appeared in London issued by the U.S. legation in that city, titled "Narrative of the Cruise of the *Alabama* by One of Her Crew." The pamphlet, put together by Consul Dudley, contained a statement by John Latham, a former crew member of the *Alabama*. According to the author, one seaman who had been recaptured after deserting was "frequently punished by having his hands and legs fastened to the rigging, the punishment being known as the 'Spread Eagle.'" The culprit "would be kept in this position for four hours . . . and this was done at least twenty times. At last they ironed his legs and arms and put him ashore on a desolate island. . . . The crew subscribed some seventeen pounds unknown to Captain Semmes, which we gave him in the hopes of its being some inducement to a vessel to take him off."[21]

Semmes was not a commander much loved by the men who served under him. Stern notes that Semmes was a poor loser. The Confederate commander continued to complain for many years after the battle that the fight between the *Alabama* and the *Kearsarge* was not a fair fight because the Yankee warship was, in fact, an ironclad. Bulloch, as the South's leading naval expert, had a more balanced account of the famous battle, writing, "Captain Winslow was quite right in doing whatever he could to increase the defensive power of his ship, and was not bound to inform his adversary that he had encased her most vulnerable parts with chain cables."[22] According to Bulloch, Winslow had fought a skillful battle.

Public opinion in North America was outraged over the British embrace of Semmes and his officers. Minister Adams continued to demand that the British government turn over Semmes and his seamen to U.S. authorities, but Russell held to his refusal to do so. Following the battle, Thomas Dudley launched an investigation into the action of the *Deerhound,* and after a brief visit to the United States during the summer, he returned with instructions from Secretary of State Seward to continue his investigation of the collusion between Semmes and the *Deerhound.*

Dudley went to France in August, where he conducted interviews with Dayton's son and the U.S. consul from Cherbourg, both of whom had observed the famous battle. Both reported witnessing communication between the *Alabama* and the *Deerhound* twice on the morning before the battle. The consul noted that the *Alabama* had taken on coal three or four days before the battle and that Semmes seemed to be waiting for someone. Dudley was convinced that the two ships had acted in concert but lacked sufficient evidence to support his belief.

In September, after he had returned to Liverpool, Dudley tracked down a seaman from the *Alabama* who testified that the night before the battle, a number of people from the *Deerhound* had come aboard the *Alabama,* and that Lancaster had spent some time alone with Semmes in his cabin. Dudley got off a deposition to Adams covering all these facts, but nothing was ever resolved, since the British refused to turn over Semmes and the rest of the Confederate sailors.

After a holiday in Europe, Semmes made his way back to the Confederate states, where he took part in the evacuation of Richmond. Semmes ended the war as an admiral and a general commanding troops in the last Appomattox campaign. The commander of the *Alabama* remained a stubborn advocate of slavery to the end of his life. Europeans, on the other hand, were impressed with the power of Union arms displayed by the sinking of the *Alabama.* As Union victories increased on land and sea, the French and English were losing whatever interest some might have had in the recognition of the Confederacy as a sovereign state.

CHAPTER 9

The Failure of Confederate Foreign Strategy

CONFEDERATE DIPLOMACY IN BRITAIN HAD BEGUN TO FALTER IN THE WINTER of 1863. In February, Bulloch reported to Mallory that he believed the British would prevent the ironclads from sailing because it was clear they were fighting ships. As a result of this conclusion, Bulloch went to France to arrange for the construction of ironclads there. He soon negotiated a contract for six warships, including two ironclads and four wooden corvettes mounting rifled cannons.

Despite Bulloch's fear that the prospect for the future construction of Confederate warships in England was dim, the official British attitude toward the Confederacy continued to follow the fortunes of war. During the spring of 1863, the Confederacy's prospects seemed good; England therefore tended to favor the South. When the news of Gettysburg and the fall of Vicksburg reached London on July 22, British leaders failed to understand the significance of these events.

On July 23, Prime Minister Palmerston declared in the House of Commons that he could not see "any distinction in principle between muskets, gunpowder, and bullets on the one side, and ships on the other." He went on to say: "Therefore I hold that on the mere ground of international law belligerents have no right to complain if merchants—I do not say the government, for that would be interference—as a mercantile transaction, supply one of the belligerents not only with arms and cannon, but also with ships destined for warlike purposes."[1] Despite the view of the prime minister, however, it was becoming increasingly difficult for the South to get its ships out of English ports.

During the spring, Confederate agents led by James Mason launched a new parliamentary campaign for recognition of the Confederacy, while at the same time organizing large public meetings calling for the recognition of the Rebel states. Southern agents and their allies in Parliament hoped to win support from the Tory opposition to the Palmerston government.

John Arthur Roebuck, a radical member of the House of Commons and a staunch Confederate ally, led the last campaign for recognition of the Confederate states. Small in stature but loud in oratory, Roebuck led an association devoted to sending material aid to the South in violation of Palmerston's policy of neutrality in the war.

Working aggressively to revive the former French initiative for a joint declaration with Britain in the recognition of the Confederacy, Roebuck forged an alliance with William Lindsay, a shipping magnate and leading member of the Confederate lobby in Parliament. Together the two men traveled to France to seek an interview with Emperor Napoleon III. Roebuck and Lindsay were granted the interview, returned to England claiming that the emperor would recognize the Confederacy, and then opened the parliamentary debate to reverse the English policy of neutrality.

As it turned out, the debate resulted in a disaster for Confederate diplomacy. The French emperor had, in fact, rejected Roebuck's proposition that France make a formal proposal to Britain of joint recognition of the Confederate states and act alone if it was declined. Roebuck delivered an offensive and intemperate speech to Parliament that was deftly countered by Henry Layard, an undersecretary to Lord Russell. Layard informed the House of Commons that no recent proposals had come from France. Reacting to this information, members of Parliament united to ridicule Roebuck and his ally Lindsay as the "amateur French Minister" and the "amateur English Ambassador." On July 13, lacking all support from the conservative opposition, Roebuck withdrew his motion for recognition of the Confederacy.[2]

Henry Hotze, the Confederate propagandist, concluded from Roebuck's defeat: "All hope of parliamentary action is past. Diplomatic means can now no longer avail, and everybody looks to Lee to conquer recognition." From his station in Paris, Slidell agreed with this view, stating that "prospects of favorable action in England appear to be hopeless."[3]

As a result of London's refusal to abandon its official policy of neutrality, Southern public opinion had now become extremely hostile to the British, the Southern press listing numerous Confederate grievances against England. Demands for retaliation were made against "the selfish and unfeeling apathy of a great Nation whose sympathies have hitherto always professedly been with a people struggling for 'constitutional liberty.'"[4] In response to the public fury against the British, the Confederate government recalled Mason, ordering him to leave England. Shortly afterward, Secretary of State Benjamin expelled the only remaining British consuls in the South, an action that completed the break between the Southern states and Britain.

After the detention of the rams, the wave of Anglophobia that swept over the South simply reflected the wreckage of Confederate foreign strategy. Jenkins notes that the "breaking of the few contacts the Confederacy had been able to maintain with Britain amounted to the public abandonment of all hope of intervention." The *Charleston Courier* commented on the recent events in England: "The open declarations of the leading journals and of the public men of that country, and, above all, the course pursued toward the steel-clad rams at Birkenhead, have caused everyone to dismiss utterly that hope."[5]

During this period, Thomas Haines Dudley was working together with Forbes and Aspinwall to perfect his espionage organization. Southern agents were still involved in the construction of warships for the Confederate navy and hoped to get some of them out. Dudley hired more detectives in northern England and Scotland, who reported directly to him. The Liverpool consul used every type of agent to gather evidence against the secret operations of the Confederacy in Britain. He recruited shipyard workers who were sympathetic to the North, professional spies, waterfront drifters, paid agents, and Confederate deserters. During the course of the war, Dudley employed over one hundred spies, none knowing the identity of another. In addition, the consul skillfully uncovered the double agents and plots of disinformation his Confederate adversaries employed against his network. As Dudley's old friend William Potts put it, "There was not a keel laid in Great Britain, without his learning the whole particulars within twenty-four hours."

Some of his agents were demanding more money. One wrote: "[I would] never undertake a job like this as I have lost all my self-respect and done myself a great deal of damage. I hope you will write by return as I am getting bankrupt. Let me know to be or not to be." Another agent, inspired by ideology, had written Dudley in the fall of 1862: "I hope sir that the First of January 1863 will do much to end the Rebellion and that the United States Government will make an example of the Rebels when they get hold of them. I will do all that I can to support the North in its great work of pulling down Slaveholding Rebels. Although I am but a mite amongst the millions of working men in this country that sympathize with the American Government, yours truly, Robert Walker."[6]

By the fall of 1863, Dudley and his detective Maguire were receiving a stream of information from all over the country, from agents who were keeping up constant surveillance on the remaining Confederate gunboats still under construction. At the same time, Dudley was coordinating the intelligence work of the American consuls in Glasgow, Dublin, Cork, and Cardiff.

Dudley and Warren Lewis Underwood, the American consul in Glasgow, kept a close watch on the Thompson Clyde Bank Iron Shipyard in Glasgow, where the Confederate cruiser *Pampero* was under construction. In the fall of 1863, when the warship was nearing completion, one of Dudley's agents, John Latham, reported that he had two Southerners up to his house but "they were so cowardly they are afraid to say anything about the vessel." A week later, Latham reported: "I fell in with a young man that has been sent down from London by one Mr. Morrey and one Mr. Anderson, Confederate Agents, and this young man knowing that I was in the Alabama let out everything about this vessel."[7]

Latham went on to report that his contact had been a captain in the Rebel army and was a good draftsman. "He was very sociable with me thinking I was a rebel same as himself. I took dinner and tea with him, after that he let me look at all the plans of the *Warrior* (a second ironclad being built in the same yard) and *Alabama*. He took me to the theatre and paid all the expenses himself." This Southern agent told Latham that he was often followed by Northern agents "but little did he think I was one he is to suspect." During the course of the Civil War, no Southern agent of consequence escaped surveillance by the efficient espionage network Dudley had established. Latham ended his report by asking, "Let me know what I shall do with this fellow?"

At the end of October, Latham reported to Maguire that he had gained some valuable information from a civil engineer "sent down from London to look at the launch of this vessel. As far as I can learn from him she is to be called the *Pampero*." He further reported that there were many Confederate officers in town. "She is getting her boilers in as fast as they can. She will be a month yet before she is ready." Latham closed by stating that he intended to take lodging in the same place as the Confederate captain of the *Pampero*.[8]

One month later, Latham, expressing the universal complaint of spies, was again grumbling to Maguire about money. "Mr. Dudley is down here but I have not seen him myself. I have not had any money from him but if there is any trouble in this matter I hope you will let me know." He reported that he was thinking of buying a suit of working clothes "to enable me to get on board of her and see what I can see."

Dudley had gone to Glasgow at the request of Ambassador Adams to seek more evidence on the *Pampero* that would meet British legal requirements. Adams wrote Dudley that it might be difficult to procure "reasonable proof of intent for warlike use by the rebels. . . . The Officials try to shelter the offenders almost everywhere." Therefore, Dudley should gather as much information as possible and turn it over to the authorities. Once again, different levels of English authority disagreed over whether the intent of the vessel under construction was peaceful. The chief constructor of the Royal Navy reported that the *Pampero* was under English ownership and was not a warship, whereas an Admiralty report supported Dudley's findings that the *Pampero* was intended as a warship. Glasgow's Emancipation Society, now an active public ally of the Northern struggle against Confederate warships built in British yards, petitioned the Foreign Office for the temporary detention of the *Pampero* until a "satisfactory investigation has been made into her character, ownership and destination." Lord Russell subsequently advised continued official surveillance of the vessel in question. British legal pettifoggery concerning hearsay evidence continued, but English sympathy for the Confederacy was on the wane.

In December, a routine investigation by government authorities discovered that the Englishmen who had ordered construction of the vessel had made a contract with Lt. George Sinclair of the Confederate States of America for the delivery of the *Pampero*. On December 10, the lord advocate of Scotland ordered that the ship be taken into custody. Four months later, the vessel was forfeited to the government for violations of the Foreign Enlistment Act. Shortly afterward, the giant ironclad named the *Warrior,* under construction by the same firm building the *Pampero,* was sold to Denmark to avoid the fate of its sister ship.[9]

Minister Adams expressed some newfound optimism in his belief that the U.S. government and Britain were coming to understand one another, and that Lord Russell was "more courteous than ever before" and his policy was becoming "more rather than less conciliatory." Adams believed that the British were at last recognizing the strength of the Union army as it won a number of significant victories on the battlefield.

Thomas Haines Dudley, on the other hand, never lost his bitterness toward the British in their official and unofficial collusion with what he referred to as the "Confederate slavocracy." Stationed as he was at the center of Southern power in Britain, the Liverpool consul daily confronted a commissioner of customs who was a Confederate agent and shipping magnates who profited from their trade with the Southern states. Dudley's careful investigations were constantly rejected by British courts on the basis of hearsay evidence. In the case of the *Pampero,* after the government had denied two Union appeals for the ship's detention, Dudley suggested to Seward that the Federal government station warships at the mouth of the Clyde to intercept the warship once it left port.

Although Dudley and Adams had won a decisive victory leading to the detention of the rams, British courts ruled against Crown lawyers who had appealed the decision in the *Alexandra* case. After losing the first appeal, the Crown moved for a second appeal, enlisting the help of Adams and Dudley to assemble witnesses and evidence. The case was then thrown out of court on a dispute over proper jurisdiction. Finally, on April 6, the case was appealed to the House of Lords, which dismissed it on technical grounds and then released the *Alexandra*. Adams wrote to Seward in reference to the original trial against the *Alexandra,* stating that "there was never such a comedy performed on a grave subject in the whole history of law."[10]

Dudley saw the final release of the *Alexandra* as proof that English laws could not prevent Confederate construction of warships in British shipyards. The Quaker lawyer, in exasperation over the action by the House of Lords, wrote:

> [The decision] is a final judgement, and leaves the verdict of the jury stand, and the ruling of Chief Baron Pollock as the correct interpretation of the Foreign Enlistment Act of this country. By this law as it now stands it is lawful for any person to build war vessels for the Confederates or any other Belligerent, to make the Guns and any other armaments, to put the guns on a tug to take the war vessel thus built into the channel three miles from land and there transfer the armament and for the vessel thus built, armed and equipped to enter upon her cruise at once.[11]

Thomas Haines Dudley continued his unremitting correspondence with members of Parliament, American congressmen, and the British and American press. Earlier he had distributed thirty thousand copies of a pamphlet describing the suffering of Union prisoners in Southern jails and camps. On January 24, 1864, Dudley received a letter from Sen. Charles Sumner who wrote: "I have been grateful for your earnest and competent watchfulness. Yours has been a difficult post. At last we are permitted to believe that England will not make war on us. I am indebted to you for the volume containing the reports of the earlier *Alexandra* case. This war can but have one end. The Rebellion will be crushed and slavery abolished."[12]

Dudley was convinced that the only way to stop Confederate naval operations in England was for the Union to rely on its "Navy and not on the justice of the English government or people." He urged that the fastest and most powerful warships in the Federal navy, commanded by the best officers in the service, be stationed off the French and English coasts. Seward did not, however, believe he could divert more ships from the navy's main work of blockading the Southern coasts, and apparently thought that the presence of the USS *Kearsarge* and a few other Union warships could meet the requirements demanded by Dudley.

John Bright, key friend of the North in the British Parliament, understood Dudley's doubt that England would ever fully enforce its own Foreign Enlistment Act. He wrote to Dudley on September 5, 1864, attempting to cheer up the dispirited consul: "If Atlanta should fall, I think the 'peace party' [referring to the Democratic Party in the United States] would find few friends in the North. . . . You are generally rather nervous and from anxiety perhaps you take a gloomy view of things." Bright wrote Dudley again on September 24, stating that he was much obliged for the book of poetry and the diplomatic correspondence Dudley had sent him. "The news seems to me to improve, and I always think of you when there is anything of a cheerful character from the States."[13] Perhaps the tireless Liverpool consul was underestimating the effectiveness of his own espionage network targeted at Confederate secret operations in Britain.

His able adversary, James Dunwoody Bulloch, however, clearly understood the damage to his own operations that Dudley's skilled network had achieved. By February 1864, James North, the main Confederate agent in Scotland, was literally driven out of the country because of exposure by Dudley's agents. Bulloch wrote bitterly to Secretary of the Confederate Navy Mallory in Richmond that Dudley's spies were making his own work impossible. Once their clandestine operations were thoroughly compromised, Confederate agents in Britain abandoned all hope of getting ironclads out of the country and recommended that no other contracts for new ironclads be entered into.[14]

At the same time, the Palmerston cabinet finally took the matter of Confederate naval construction in England out of the hands of the courts. Dudley benefited from a new spirit of cooperation by English authorities in his continuing investigation of the Confederate warships *Alexandra* and *Georgia*. The latter ship had been first built as a merchant vessel when the seven-hundred-ton screw steamer was bought by the Rebels and converted into a cruiser at Dumbarton, Scotland, in March 1863. After escaping, the *Georgia* raided Union commercial ships for more than a year, when at the end of April 1864, flying the English flag, it steamed into Liverpool for refitting. Dudley, with his usual efficiency, put the Rebel cruiser under surveillance.[15]

Finding that the costs of refitting were too high, the Rebels put the ship up for sale. The *Georgia* was then purchased by a wealthy Liverpool shipowner, who claimed that he would convert the ship into a merchantman. Dudley believed this was a ruse and sent Adams a full file on the *Georgia*. After Adams complained to Lord Russell and warned that Rebel cruisers

under English ownership could lead to a break in American and English relations, Russell ordered that no belligerent warship could enter British ports.
Dudley then provided the Federal navy with exact details of the *Georgia's* sailing orders. The Rebel cruiser steamed out of Liverpool on August 11, was
captured by the USS *Niagara* on the fifteenth, and then was sent to Boston as
a Union prize. Thomas Haines Dudley was destroying the Confederate navy
one ship at a time.

In July 1864, Dudley learned that the recently released *Alexandra* had
been purchased by Henry Lafone, a Confederate agent who then converted
the ship into a blockade runner and renamed it the *Mary*. When the former
Alexandra, on July 17, sailed for Nassau, where Dudley expected it to be
armed by the Rebels, the spymaster forwarded his usual thorough briefing on
the ship to Union authorities in the West Indies. The Federal consul in Nassau, by using Dudley's information, forced the British to act. The ship was
seized on December 13 and held until the end of the war.

During the remaining months of the war, only one other Confederate
raider escaped from England. This was the *Sea King*, later renamed the
Shenandoah, which escaped from the port of London, a port under the jurisdiction of Consul Morse. Since there were few Northern merchant ships flying
the American flag now sailing in the Atlantic, Secretary of the Confederate
Navy Mallory had ordered Bulloch to outfit a cruiser for the Pacific to hunt
down and destroy the New England whaling fleet in arctic waters. Bulloch
subsequently located a full-rigged ship with auxillary steam power named the
Sea King, which he bought and refitted as a cruiser. Though the Federal
authorities were aware of this new Confederate cruiser, Bulloch got the ship
out using his standard ruses. On October 8, 1864, the *Sea King* left the port of
London unarmed, followed by a tender, the *Laurel*, which on October 18
transferred guns and ammunition to the new cruiser at Funchal, Madeira.
Dudley had been keeping a close watch on the screw steamer *Laurel* when it
docked at Liverpool. He learned that its officers were taking orders from
Fraser, Trenholm and Company, and that she had been cleared for Matamoros
by the Confederate agent Henry Lafone. Dudley reported correctly that the
Laurel would transfer seamen and arms to the *Sea King*.[16]

Dudley was once again angered at the escape of a new Confederate warship and wrote Seward stating that if Federal warships had been on station at
the mouth of the Thames, the *Sea King* could have been captured. In any case,
Lt. James I. Waddell took command of the *Shenandoah* and for a time sailed
the ship shorthanded because of difficulty in enlisting a crew. He succeeded,
however, in recruiting enough seamen from the ships he soon captured.

Sailing around the Cape of Good Hope, the *Shenandoah* reached Melbourne, Australia, on January 25, 1865. After a number of desertions and threats by Northern sympathizers in Australia, Waddell was able to recruit new crew members. Subsequently, the *Shenandoah* set out on its long cruise to destroy Yankee whalers. On April 1, the *Shenandoah* surprised, captured, and burned four whaling ships at Ascension Island in the eastern Carolines. During the two weeks that the Confederate raider remained at Ascension Island, General Lee surrendered his armies at Appomattox, an event unknown to Captain Waddell and his crew. Leaving the Carolines on April 13, the *Shenandoah* set sail for the Arctic Ocean, reaching the Bering Straits on June 16, a month after the Civil War ended.[17]

The *Shenandoah* rapidly succeeded in destroying the entire Yankee whaling fleet. From June 22 to 28, the last Confederate cruiser afloat captured twenty-four ships and burned all but four, which were used for transporting hundreds of prisoners. When one of the captains of the captured whaling ships told Waddell that the war was over, the Confederate commander refused to believe him. After capturing a ship from San Francisco, however, Waddell learned from recent newspapers of Lee's surrender and the fact that the war was still continuing under General Johnson. He further discovered that President Jefferson Davis had issued a proclamation stating that the war was to be prosecuted with "renewed vigor." Waddell, determined to carry on the war all by himself, captured nineteen more ships in five days.

After battering its way through the ice floes of the Bering Straits, the *Shenandoah* headed south, where Waddell planned to run into San Francisco Bay to capture a Federal ironclad at anchor, to be followed by a demand for ransom from the city. On August 2, the *Shenandoah* met the British bark *Baracouta*, carrying recent newspapers from San Francisco. These reports finally convinced Waddell that the war was over. He stored his guns below decks, disarmed the crew, and made the decision to sail his ship seventeen thousand miles to Liverpool.[18]

After circumnavigating the world, the *Shenandoah* entered the Mersey River on November 5, 1865, where she hauled down the Confederate flag and surrendered the ship to British authorities. The *Shenandoah* thus ended a fifty-eight-thousand-mile cruise, having captured thirty-eight ships and destroyed thirty-two.

Historical justice appears to have been served when the last of the Confederate raiders was turned over to the U.S. consul at Liverpool, Thomas Haines Dudley, the man who had devoted the best years of his life to the destruction of the Confederate navy. Dudley put the *Shenandoah* up for auction, and it was bought by the sultan of Zanzibar. At the war's end, the Quaker spymaster had given precise sailing dates and cargo manifests for 324 blockade steamers, 126 of which were either captured or destroyed, and had been instrumental in stopping or making ineffective twelve Confederate warships forming the backbone of the Confederate navy.[19]

The cornerstone of the South's strategic plan for victory in its war with the North had been British recognition and intervention in the North American conflict to ensure the permanent division of the Republic. Without British intervention, the cause of the South was lost.

Historians have long debated the reasons for the refusal of Britain to intervene in the American Civil War. Among the most plausible explanations must be Britain's fear of the loss of Canada to Union armies; London's concern about undermining the principle of maritime rights of neutrals, which could be turned against Britain in the future when a Northern fleet of "*Alabamas*" might sweep the seas of English merchant ships; and the belief that Britain's major national interests lay in the European theater. In the final view, France posed a greater threat to Britain than did the United States.

The historical record reveals that both Palmerston and Russell were tempted to intervene in the American conflict but were restrained by the coalition of Whigs, liberals, and radicals upon which political survival of the cabinet rested. Palmerston, famous for his statement that Britain had no eternal friends and no eternal enemies but only eternal interests, was the great nineteenth-century practitioner of realpolitik. His foremost concern proved to be expediency rather than principle; he proved himself capable of having second thoughts on decisions that bore great risk.

Moreover, both Palmerston and Russell had to face the turn in public opinion brought about by Lincoln's Emancipation Proclamation and the fact that in the final analysis, the South bore the stigma of slavery. Finally, it was British working-class support for the Northern cause of freedom and democracy, and the rise of the Emancipation Society, that carried the day in British public opinion.

Although Union armies proved the final determinant in the defeat of the South, a skillful combination of diplomacy, espionage, and propaganda by William Seward, Charles Francis Adams, and Thomas Dudley prevented the Confederacy from carrying out its strategic war plan in Europe.

CHAPTER 10

Consul Dudley Stays On

DURING THE FINAL MONTHS OF THE WAR, THE AMERICAN CONSUL AT LIVER-pool continued the same unflagging pace of work that he had established from the day he took office. Dudley had become the leading expert on Confederate operations in England. His advice was sought by American congressmen, British members of Parliament, U.S. naval authorities, and public officials of all kinds. He provided John Bright with material for his parliamentary speeches; dispatched information on the Confederate ship *Georgia* to Richard Dana, the U.S. attorney for the district of Massachusetts; and sent more data to the State Department to assist in the prosecution of its case against the Confederate ship *Peterhoff*, which had been seized by the Federal navy. Dudley continued his unremitting propaganda work by distributing pamphlets, copies of speeches, and diplomatic correspondence to leading politicians in England.

All of the special agents sent to England during the war, including Evarts, Forbes, and Aspinwall, sought out Dudley for information and advice. Benjamin Moran wrote to Dudley after one of the consul's visits to London: "You have given us more facts in this note about vessels in the Clyde than we ever got from all other sources combined." Moran, referring to the Liverpool consul, wrote in his diary that "none but an iron man could stand such awful wear."[1]

In July 1864, a typical note from Moran to Dudley read: "Please let me know the present name of the ship once called the *Emily St. Pierre* and where she is, if possible. And also any facts at command about the *Sumter, Japan, Alexandra, Agrippina, A. D. Vance, Eugenie,* or any vessels that actually belong to the rebels." When Capt. John Winslow of the USS *Kearsarge* wrote to

Minister Adams requesting that Adams and Dayton, U.S. minister in Paris, issue instructions to all U.S. consuls to inform him of Confederate ship movements, Adams replied: "To Mr. Dudley there is no need of. No advice is necessary for him."

After listing Dudley's multiple activities during the war, Brainard Dyer, in his biographical essay, notes that "all of these activities growing out of the war were in addition to Dudley's normal consular duties, duties which in March 1864 the State Department informed him he had 'conducted with admirable prudence, and with a regard to the interests of the United States deserving of high commendation and imitation.'"[2]

When the war ended, Dudley, chronically ill and weary from his war labors, wished to resign his post and return to the practice of law in New Jersey. The State Department, however, aware of the Liverpool consul's encyclopedic knowledge of Confederate assets in Britain, turned down his request to retire from his post and assigned him the task of disposing of Confederate property. Dudley accepted the new assignment and promptly entered a claim as property of the United States all the Confederate ships that had sought refuge in Liverpool, including the *Shenandoah,* the *Tallahassee,* the *Sumter,* and the *Rappahannock.* He subsequently sold all these ships, as well as Confederate munitions and other military supplies that he located throughout the British Isles. Considerable amounts of money were soon transferred to the U.S. Treasury. Dudley realized £17,000 from the sale of the *Shenandoah* alone, and sent forty-seven chronometers and a sextant taken from the ships captured by the *Shenandoah* back to the United States. At the same time, Dudley instituted a lawsuit against Fraser, Trenholm and Company for the recovery of large amounts of Southern cotton it was holding.

Dudley recalls that in the last month of the war, he was approached by James Bains of Manchester, who was a friend of John Bright and a great admirer of Abraham Lincoln. Bains, who wished to present a marble bust of Bright to Mr. Lincoln, asked Dudley if he would send the gift to the president. Dudley remembers: "The bust arrived at my office in Liverpool on the day we received the sad intelligence of Mr. Lincoln's assassination. I wrote to Mr. Bains, and asked him, now that Lincoln was dead, what I should do with the bust. He replied, 'Give it to the people of the United States.' And I forwarded it to Washington; and this bust now stands somewhere in the White House, probably without a history or so much as a name attached to it to tell who it is."[3]

Once again, in May 1868, Consul Dudley asked to be relieved from his post, and once again Secretary of State Seward asked him to remain to carry on urgent postwar activities. By 1871, Dudley had served nearly ten years as consul to Liverpool. His health was poor, and he again submitted his resignation. The State Department again refused his resignation, asking him to remain one more year to assist in the preparation of the American case in the international arbitration of the *Alabama* claims against the British.

Without Dudley, who, over a number of years, had meticulously built up the case for reparations from Britain for the depredations by the *Alabama* against American merchant ships, the United States would have had no case. During the whole course of the cruise of the *Alabama,* the tireless consul had met every shipmaster and crewman from ships sunk by the Confederate raider to take depositions and create a file for damages against Great Britain for its responsibility in the construction and escape of the South's most famous cruiser.

Secretary of State Seward, Minister Adams, and Consul Dudley all carefully prepared the case against Britain for claims against the Confederate cruisers built in British shipyards. Seward postponed American claims against Britain during the war, while emphasizing that such claims were just and would be revived. Lord Russell, in the last year of the war, summarized the British position on American claims for indemnity for the depredations of Confederate cruisers built in Britain. Russell believed that under proper circumstances, the issue might be submitted to the arbitration of a friendly power. The foreign minister did not wish to submit to American bullying, however, and warned that to give ground on the *Alabama* claims would bring "no limit to the concessions demanded" by Washington. Over a period of years, the British refused to negotiate the issue.[4]

Once peace had been established on the North American continent, Minister Adams still worried about hostile relations between the two countries, warning Washington that it was not yet time to press claims for indemnity against Britain. Tension between the two countries existed over several serious issues: Canada, which had given sanctuary to Confederate soldiers escaping from Union prisons; and attacks on Vermont and New York by Confederate agents during the final months of the war.

In 1866, the Fenians, an organization of Irish-Americans, launched a series of armed raids on Canada with the aim of holding the country hostage until the British granted Ireland full independence. Since the British had rejected Seward's effort to settle American claims against Britain for its support of Confederate sea raiders, many Americans believed that support for the Fenian attacks on Canada would make Britain more amenable to negotiations. In January 1869, Britain and the United States signed the Johnson-Clarendon Convention for arbitrating all claims between the two countries. Although the treaty served as a peaceful solution to the issue of the Confederate raiders, it contained no apology by Britain for releasing the cruisers nor provision for indirect damage they had caused in prolonging the war. As a result, the Senate under the leadership of Charles Sumner rejected the treaty by a vote of fifty-four to one.

Sumner then began to argue for indirect claims of well over $2 billion for the prolongation of the war by the Confederate raiders and demanded that Britain withdraw from Canada. The famous radical Republican castigated England for its almost universal sympathy with the slaveholders' rebellion, for granting "belligerent rights to the rebels, in building them a navy, in fitting out cruisers to sweep our commerce from the seas, in furnishing arms and ammunitions to their army, and supplies to clothe and feed them."

Because of this sympathy for the South, Sumner argued: "You can also understand why one of the leading blockade runners, whilst mainly engaged in the blockade business, was elected Mayor of Liverpool; why John Laird could be elected to Parliament from Birkenhead by an increased majority; and why Sheffield, a leading manufacturing town, trading with the United States, would send Roebuck as their representative."

Sumner was convinced that the "effect of all this was to prolong, to intensify and render more bloody the war. . . . But for this recognition, the South could not have had a cruiser on the ocean. . . . It was the hope of intervention that buoyed up the South, and cheered them on in the desperate contest."[5] The senator concluded that without British support, the war could not have lasted more than a year. This fiery speech served once more to increase the tensions between the two countries to new postwar heights.

Minister Adams remained at his post in London until April 1, 1868. During his final months in Great Britain, he unsuccessfully attempted to get the British to agree to negotiate American wartime claims. Adams's tact and diplomatic skill during his tenure in London had served America well. He became known for his thoughtful moderation, dignified good temper, caution, and perseverence. He won the respect of Lord Russell and most of the other major British leaders during his years in London. As John Bright once put it, Adams had never been "in a passion and never in a panic." Adams and Consul Dudley had made a good team in the crucial matter of the construction of Confederate warships in Britain. Dudley provided the facts, and Adams knew how to present them. After the spring of 1868, Dudley remained in Liverpool amassing his files on wartime Confederate activities, while Adams returned to his home in Massachusetts, where he spent an uneventful few years.

In the interim, the outbreak of war between France and Prussia forced Britain to seek an accommodation with the United States, and after a short period of negotiations, the two countries signed the Treaty of Washington on

Adams himself was generally credited in the American press with a diplomatic triumph and for having singlehandedly saved the negotiations, which had more than once threatened to break up. Even members of the British cabinet praised Charles Francis Adams for "the dignity, tact, self-command, and moderation" with which he had fulfilled his functions as arbitrator. The drama of the secret operations of the Confederacy in Great Britain thus came to an end. But it must be remembered that the fate of the Confederacy had been to a great extent decided on the seas and in the foreign ministries of Europe. As Philip Van Doren Stern notes, "The Union blockade, the loss of one seaport after another, and the witholding of recognition by foreign countries did more to defeat the South than anything its armies could ever do to offset these crippling blows."

His labors completed, Thomas Haines Dudley's resignation was finally accepted by the State Department in the fall of 1872. The Liverpool consul returned to the practice of law in New Jersey. His formidable Confederate adversary during the war, James Dunwoody Bulloch, went into business in Liverpool and remained in England as a forgotten man of the Confederacy for the rest of his life.

Stern ranks Bulloch with Lee as one of the great Southern war leaders, writing:

> Bulloch was worth more to the South than a regiment of minor military officers whose names are much better known than his. Jefferson Davis, whose chief contribution to the war was a ponderous mass of turgid prose, is remembered while Bulloch, the secret operator, the ingenious planner, the good technician, the astute businessman, the honest administrator of huge funds, the man who was responsible for the most effective moves his government made beyond its borders, remains almost unknown.[8]

Yet history records that the secret operations of the most skillful Confederate agent in Britain were hamstrung and eventually nullified by Thomas Haines Dudley, the Quaker spymaster stationed in Liverpool.

Samuel Price Edwards, the collector of customs at Liverpool and a valuable Confederate ally throughout the war, ended his career in disgrace. A notorious cotton speculator during the course of the war, Edwards was sued in 1867 by Liverpool cotton brokers for reneging on an order to purchase cotton. He was subsequently convicted of perjury, then admitted his guilt, and the case was dropped. However, Dudley got one of the cotton brokers who had sued Edwards to sign an affidavit declaring that Edwards had been "a

May 8, 1871, a treaty approved by the Senate before the end of the m
This agreement called for an international tribunal of five arbitrators to r
the *Alabama* claims; provided for settlement of a dispute over the Sar
Islands; established commercial reciprocity between Canada and the U
States; and resolved a dispute over Canadian fisheries on the Atlantic

President Ulysses S. Grant, succumbing to public pressure, ever
appointed Charles Francis Adams as the American arbitrator for the *Al*
claims. Adams, together with his son Brooks, set sail for Europe in No\
1871. In the meantime, Consul Dudley had worked tirelessly durir
period gathering new evidence and affidavits for preparation of the U.
ernment case in the arbitration of the *Alabama* claims, evidence that (
Francis Adams would use for his arguments against Britain. Dudley
went to Geneva to assist in preparing the American claims. The cas\
United States in the *Alabama* claims arbitration referred more than
the efforts of "our energetic Consul at Liverpool," while the British c
case recognized "the American Consul at Liverpool, whose activity in
for secret information appears to have been indefatigable."

The Treaty of Washington arbitration proceedings opened in Ge
December 15, 1871. After a brief two-day session, the tribunal was ac
until June 15 so that Britain could present its counter to the America
The British had been unpleasantly surprised that the American
included its indirect claims covering losses resulting from the tr
American ships to the British flag, increased rates of insurance d\
threat of Confederate raiders, and the prolongation of the war by th
ern warships built in Britain. Meanwhile, Adams returned to Massacl
await the reopening of the arbitration proceedings in six months.

After a long and complex debate in the British cabinet over the
of the British countercase against the *Alabama* claims, the interna!
bunal reconvened on June 15. Following considerable negotiation
promise by both sides, the Americans dropped their indirect claim
tribunal dismissed British liability for damage caused by the *Georg*
ville, Sumter, and other smaller Southern raiders. The tribunal he
responsible and liable for the damage caused by the *Alabama, Fl*
Shenandoah, however, and ordered Britain to pay $15.5 million to t
States as liability for the damage done by the Confederate cruisers t
British Isles.[7]

There were, of course, members of Parliament who complaine
"enormous" indemnity Britain was forced to pay, and Americans wl
the settlement was much too small. But Adams considered the jud
sonable and all that could be expected under the circumstances.

warm sympathizer with the Confederates and their cause" throughout the war and had colluded in the escape of the *Alabama*. As a result, Edwards was dismissed from his job. Bulloch, who had worked closely with Edwards, remarked that the collector of customs went rapidly downhill after the perjury scandal and his dismissal from office.

Thomas Haines Dudley, on the other hand, left his post with great honor. On his return to New Jersey, the consul built a large house on an estate he had purchased near his boyhood home in Camden, became a prominent member of the New Jersey bar, and carried on his lifelong role in the Republican Party. Dudley had kept his hand in politics during his tenure in Liverpool by returning to participate in the 1864 and 1868 Republican presidential campaigns. Throughout his life, he retained his reputation as an expert on protectionist trade policies, and in 1867, he was assigned by Secretary of State Seward to accompany the economist David Wells on a tour of Europe for the purpose of investigating conditions of production and labor in England, France, Belgium, and Germany. On his visit home from Liverpool in 1868, a dinner had been given for him in Newark for recognition of his distinguished services to the country. The dinner was attended by Supreme Court Justice Bradley, Senators Frelinghuysen and Cattal, Attorney General Robeson, and other distinguished guests.[9]

Dudley entertained President Grant and his family on his new estate and soon was enlisted in the new corporate elite. The former Liverpool consul became president of the Pittsburgh, Titusville and Buffalo Railroad and the New Jersey Mining Company, and served on the boards of the Camden and Atlantic Railroad, the West Jersey Railroad, the Camden and Philadelphia Ferry Company, and the People's Gaslight Company of New Jersey. He was elected president of the Bar Association of Camden and the first vice president of the American Protective Tariff League.

Dudley's prominent role in spreading the gospel of American protectionism fit naturally into his lifelong anti-British philosophy, a view reinforced by his wartime experience in England. He never forgave the British for their collusion with the Confederacy and, as such, reflected the attitude of the small band of Americans huddled together in the hostile environment of London and Liverpool during the war. It was a view expressed by Benjamin Moran, who wrote Dudley in 1864: "I agree with you about the shameless course of this gov't. from the beginning, and when the day of reckoning comes, if I should be alive, I hope I shall be oblivious of mercy towards this gov't. As usual, they will whine and sniffle for kind treatment and bring up the old Boston twaddle about the same Shakespeare, the same Milton, the same race and the same language."[10]

The Quaker lawyer from New Jersey was a product of his time. As an abolitionist and Free Soiler he played a major role in the great radical Republican Revolution that resulted in the overthrow of the feudal slave system of the Southern states. After the war, he remained active in the Republican-led wave of capitalist development that within thirty-five years would make the United States the leading industrial country in the world. History does not reveal what he thought of the postwar Grant administration scandals, the wild speculative excess of the Gilded Age, or the emergence of the robber barons who created the corporate trusts of the late nineteenth century.

We do know, however, that the tall, sober lawyer from New Jersey retained his own stern sense of responsibility until the end of his life. An eminent member of the New Jersey bar described Dudley "as a lawyer, distinguished for the absolute devotion to the cause of his client with which he conducted his cases; no difficulty daunted and no obstacle deterred him. He persevered with indomitable energy and unceasing assiduity until his object was obtained."[11] These were the same personality traits that had characterized his struggle against the Confederate navy.

On the morning of April 15, 1893, Thomas Haines Dudley, upon arrival at the Broad Street Station in Philadelphia, died of a massive heart attack. He was seventy-three years old. Despite his postwar achievements, no period of his life could ever match the years of duty as consul in Liverpool, when his contribution to the war against the Confederacy equaled that of the best Union generals in the field.

NOTES

INTRODUCTION

1. Allan Nevins, *War for the Union* (New York: Charles Scribner's Sons, 1960), vol. 2, 242. American historians recently have returned to the view of the American Civil War as an international event. See Robert E. May, ed., *The Union, the Confederacy, and the Atlantic Rim* (South Bend, Indiana: Purdue University Press, 1955).
2. Bernard Bailyn, *The Peopling of British North America* (New York: Vintage Books, 1988), 5.
3. Richard Hofstadter, William Miller, and David Aaron, *The United States: The History of a Republic,* 2nd ed. (Englewood Cliffs, NJ: Prentice-Hall, 1967), 97.
4. See H. H. Peckham, *The Colonial Wars, 1689–1762* (Chicago: University of Chicago Press, 1964).
5. "The Present and Probable Future of the Three Races That Inhabit the Territory of the United States," chap. 17 in Alexis de Tocqueville, *Democracy in America,* vol. 1 (New York: Modern Library, 1981), 200–201.
6. James M. McPherson, "The Whole Family of Man: Lincoln and the Best Hope Abroad," in May, *Union, Confederacy, and Atlantic Rim,* 131–32.
7. James McPherson, *Battle Cry of Freedom: The Civil War Era* (New York: Oxford University Press, 1988), 565.
8. Howard Jones, *Union in Peril: The Crisis over British Intervention in the Civil War* (Chapel Hill, North Carolina: University of North Carolina Press, 1992), 4.

9. Quoted by May, *Union, Confederacy, and Atlantic Rim*, 2.

10. Seward to Charles Adams, July 28, 1862. Quoted by Howard Jones, "History and Mythology: The Crisis over British Intervention in the Civil War," in May, *Union, Confederacy and Atlantic Rim*, 35.

11. Norman A. Graebner, "Northern Diplomacy and European Neutrality," in *Why the North Won the Civil War*, ed. David Donald (New York: Collier, 1960), 60–61.

12. Jones, *Union in Peril*, 3.

13. Ibid., 16.

14. Brian Jenkins, *Britain and the War for the Union* (Montreal: McGill-Queens University Press, 1980), vol. 2, 1.

15. Ibid., 19.

16. See Norman Ferris, *The Trent Affair: A Diplomatic Crisis* (Knoxville: University of Tennessee Press, 1977).

17. Dudley to Seward, May 10, 1862, Thomas Haines Dudley Collection, Huntington Library, San Marino, California, box 1, DU-4573 (Dudley Collection hereafter cited by DU number).

18. The South's top foreign agent tells his own story in James D. Bulloch, *The Secret Service of the Confederate States in Europe; or, How the Confederate Cruisers Were Equipped*, 2 vols. (New York: Thomas Yoseloff, 1959).

19. Jones, *Union in Peril*, 28.

20. Douglas H. Maynard, "Union Efforts to Prevent the Escape of the *Alabama*," *Mississippi Valley Historical Review* 41, no. 1 (June 1954): 42.

21. DU-4573, Dudley to Seward, January 16, 1863.

22. Jenkins, *Britain and the War*, vol. 2, 179–81.

23. For the Lincoln cabinet's debate on emancipation, see McPherson, *Battle Cry of Freedom*, 502–5.

24. Jones, *Union in Peril*, 187.

25. Ibid., 176.

26. Jenkins, *Britain and the War*, vol. 2, 179–81.

27. See Thomas H. Dudley, "Three Critical Periods in Our Diplomatic Relations with England during the Late War: Personal Recollections of Thomas H. Dudley, Late United States Consul at Liverpool," *Pennsylvania Magazine of History and Biography* 17, no. 1 (1893).

28. Jenkins, *Britain and the War*, vol. 2, 196–97.

29. Douglas H. Maynard, "The Forbes-Aspinwall Mission," *Mississippi Valley Historical Review* 45, no. 1 (June 1958): 75.

30. Thomas Hansard, ed., *Hansard's Parliamentary Debates*, 3rd ser. (London: T. C. Hansard, 1831–91), vol. 170, 33–39.

31. Quoted by Jenkins, *Britain and the War*, vol. 2, 255.

32. Quoted by D. Crook, *The North, the South and the Powers, 1861–1865* (New York: Wiley, 1974), 326.
33. Dudley, "Three Critical Periods," 53.
34. See Jenkins, *Britain and the War,* vol. 2, chap. 11, for a detailed analysis of the high-level British resolution of the rams crisis.
35. See "Case of the United States before the Tribunal of Arbitration at Geneva," in *Papers Relating to the Treaty of Washington,* vol. 1 (Washington, D.C.: U.S. Government Printing Office, 1972).
36. Nevins, *War for the Union,* vol. 2, 242.

CHAPTER 1: THE SECOND AMERICAN REVOLUTION

1. McPherson, *Battle Cry of Freedom,* 115–16.
2. Eric Foner, *Free Soil, Free Labor, Free Men: The Ideology of the Republican Party before the Civil War* (New York: Oxford University Press, 1970), 313.
3. Ibid., 223.
4. George E. Baker, ed., *The Works of William H. Seward,* 5 vols. (New York: Houghton, Mifflin and Co., 1884) vol. 4, 302.
5. John A. May and Joan R. Faust, *South Carolina Secedes* (New York: Columbia University Press, 1960), 88–89.
6. Frederick W. Seward, *Reminiscences of a Wartime Statesman and Diplomat, 1830–1815* (New York: Putnam's and Sons, 1916), 147.
7. William Howard Russell, *My Diary North and South* (Boston: Bunham, 1863), 93.
8. Jenkins, *Britain and the War,* vol. 2, 30.
9. Frederick Bancroft, *The Life of William H. Seward,* 2 vols. (New York: Harper and Brothers, 1900), vol. 2, 62–63.
10. Carl Schurz, *The Reminiscences of Carl Schurz,* 3 vols. (New York: The McClure Company, 1907), vol. 2, 245.
11. William John Potts, "Biographical Sketch of the Late Hon. Thomas H. Dudley," a paper read before the American Philosophical Society, Philadelphia, April 19, 1895, reprinted from *Proceedings of the American Philosophical Society* 34 (June 4, 1895), 3–36.
12. *New York Herald,* March 17, 1856, 1.
13. Potts, "Thomas H. Dudley," 8.
14. Allan Nevins, "The Nomination of Abraham Lincoln: New Forces and New Men," address delivered at the Chicago Historical Society on May 18, 1960, reprinted by Chicago Historical Society, 1960, 1.
15. Ibid., 1–2.
16. Hofstadter, Miller, and Aaron, *United States,* 403.

17. Details of the nominating process given by Thomas H. Dudley, "The Inside Facts of Lincoln's Nomination," *Century Magazine* (1890), reprinted in *Civil War History* 1, no. 1 (March 1995), 477–79.
18. Potts, "Thomas H. Dudley," 10.
19. Ibid., 11.
20. Brainard Dyer, "Thomas H. Dudley," *Civil War History* 1, no. 4 (December 1955), 402.
21. Sarah A. Wallace and Francis E. Gillespie, eds., *The Journal of Benjamin Moran*, 2 vols. (Chicago: University of Chicago Press, 1949), 832–33.
22. DU-1275.
23. Ibid.

CHAPTER 2: THE BALANCE OF POWER

1. E. J. Hobsbawm, *The Age of Capital, 1848–1875* (New York: Pantheon, 1975), 78.
2. *Congressional Globe*, 36th Congress, part 1, 102.
3. Hansard, *Parliamentary Debates,* vol. 167, 1378–79.
4. David Herbert Donald, *Charles Sumner and the Rights of Man* (New York: Knopf, 1970), 21.
5. Jenkins, *Britain and the War*, vol. 1, 104.
6. Ephraim D. Adams, *Great Britain and the American Civil War*, 2 vols. (New York: Russell and Russell, 1925), vol 1, 106.
7. Jenkins, *Britain and the War*, vol. 1, 154.
8. Ibid., 172.
9. Ibid., 174.
10. Ferris, *Trent Affair*, 22.
11. Ibid., 25.
12. Herman Melville, *Redburn: His First Voyage* (Boston: St. Botolphe Society, 1924), 161.
13. DU-4573.
14. Ibid.
15. Ibid.
16. Jenkins, *Britain and the War*, vol. 1, 211–12
17. Ibid.
18. Ferris, *Trent Affair*, 47.
19. Ibid., 180.
20. Ibid., 182.
21. Ibid., 184.
22. Ibid., 185. Also Crook, *North, South and Powers*, 131–33.

23. Jenkins, *Britain and the War,* vol. 1, 227.
24. Dudley, "Three Critical Periods," 36–39.
25. Ibid.

CHAPTER 3: A NEST OF PIRATES

1. McPherson, *Battle Cry of Freedom,* 314–15.
2. Neil Fred Sanders, "Lincoln's Consuls in the British Isles, 1861–1865" (Ph.D. diss., University of Missouri, 1971), 26.
3. Ibid., 33.
4. DU-4573, Wilding to Adams, July 3, 1861.
5. Ibid., Wilding to Adams, September 12, 1861.
6. Ibid., Wilding to Adams, September 20, 1861.
7. Sanders, "Lincoln's Consuls," 35.
8. Ibid., 33.
9. Ibid., 40.
10. Ibid., 41.
11. Ibid., 44.
12. Potts, "Thomas H. Dudley," 13, 19.
13. DU-4573.
14. DU-3557.
15. DU-1486.
16. DU-4573.
17. Ibid., Dudley to Seward, February 3, 1862.
18. Ibid., Dudley to Adams, February 15, 1862, February 17, 1862.
19. Ibid., Dudley to Adams, March 16, 1862.
20. Bulloch, *Secret Service,* vol. 1, 227.

CHAPTER 4: THE ESCAPE OF THE CONFEDERATE CRUISERS

1. See Philip Van Doren Stern, *When the Guns Roared: World Aspects of the American Civil War* (Garden City, NY: Doubleday & Co., 1965), 150–51.
2. Bulloch, *Secret Service,* vol. 1, 152–53.
3. Ibid., 159–60. The full correspondence beween Bulloch and Confederate officials can be found in *Official Records of the Union and Confederate Navies in the War of the Rebellion* (hereafter cited as *ORN*), 30 vols. (Washington, D.C.: U.S. Government Printing Office, 1894–1922).
4. Jenkins, *Britain and the War,* vol. 2, 126–27.
5. DU-4573, Dudley to Adams, May 23, 1862.
6. Ibid., Dudley to Seward, May 22, 1862.
7. Ibid., Wilding to Dudley, July 3, 1862.

8. Ibid., Dudley to Wilding, July 4, 1862.
9. Ibid., Dudley to Seward, July 25, 1862.
10. Ibid., Dudley to Seward, May 21, 1862.
11. Ibid., Seward to Dudley, June 4, 1862.
12. Ibid., Seward to Dudley, July 10, 1862.
13. DU-4213, Wilding to Dudley, June 19, 1862.
14. Maynard, "Union Efforts," 47.
15. Ibid., 49.
16. Ibid.
17. Box 16, Dudley Collection, Huntington Library.
18. Maynard, "Union Efforts," 52.
19. Jenkins, *Britain and the War,* vol. 2, 121–25.
20. Bulloch, *Secret Service,* vol. 1, 229–31.
21. DU-4481, Yonge to Dudley, July 28, 1862.
22. Bulloch, *Secret Service,* vol. 1, 236–37.
23. Ibid., 238.
24. Ibid., 239–40.
25. Maynard, "Union Efforts," 58.
26. Bulloch, *Secret Service,* vol. 1, 241.
27. Ibid., 242.
28. Wallace and Gillespie, *Moran Journal,* vol. 2, 1048.
29. Bulloch, *Secret Service,* vol. 1, 255.

CHAPTER 5: THE PIRATES AT WORK

1. For details of the cruise of the *Florida,* see *ORN.*
2. Quoted by Philip Van Doren Stern, *The Confederate Navy: A Pictorial History* (New York: Bonanza Books, 1962), 116.
3. Bulloch, *Secret Service,* vol. 1, 254–56; Bulloch to Mallory, September 10, 1862.
4. DU-4573, Dudley to Seward, September 2, 1862.
5. Ibid.
6. DU-4573, Dudley to Seward, September 3, 1862.
7. Raphael Semmes, *Memoirs of Service Afloat during the War Between the States* (London: R. Bentley, 1899), 96.
8. Ibid., 128.
9. Ibid., 129–30.
10. Ibid., 131.
11. Bulloch, *Secret Service,* vol. 2, 112–13.
12. Semmes, *Memoirs,* 402.
13. Ibid., 403.

14. Ibid., 411–12.
15. Ibid., 426–27.
16. Ibid., 49l.
17. Ibid., 511–12.
18. Ibid., 523–24.
19. Ibid., 538.
20. For Semmes's account of the battle between the *Alabama* and the USS *Hatteras*, see *Memoirs*, 543–50; for the account by Lieutenant Commander Blake, captain of the *Hatteras*, see *ORN*, ser. 1, vol. 2, 18–20.
21. Semmes, *Memoirs*, 558.
22. Ibid., 559.
23. Stern, *Confederate Navy*, 128.

CHAPTER 6: THE PROPAGANDA WAR

1. Dudley, "Three Critical Periods," 40–41.
2. Ibid., 41–42.
3. Bright to Dudley, December 29, 1861, reprinted in Potts, "Thomas H. Dudley," 14.
4. G. D. Lillibridge, *Beacon of Freedom: The Impact of American Democracy upon Great Britain, 1830–1870* (Philadelphia: University of Pennsylvania Press, 1955), 111.
5. Quoted by Karl E. Meyer, "Editorial Notebook," editorial page, *New York Times*, July 5, 1993.
6. Frank L. Owsley, *King Cotton Diplomacy: Foreign Relations of the Confederate States of America*, 2nd ed. (Chicago: University of Chicago Press, 1959), 155.
7. Henry Adams, *The Education of Henry Adams: An Autobiography* (Boston: Houghton-Mifflin Company, 1918), 136–37.
8. Owsley, *King Cotton Diplomacy*, 157.
9. Ibid., 159.
10. Jenkins, *Britain and the War*, vol. 2, 51–52.
11. Ibid., 57.
12. Adams, *Britain and the Civil War*, 302–3.
13. Wallace and Gillespie, *Moran Journal*, vol. 2, 1029.
14. Jenkins, *Britain and the War*, vol. 2, 167.
15. Jones, *Union in Peril*, 163.
16. Ibid., 172.
17. Stern, *When the Guns Roared*, 154.
18. DU-315, Bright to Dudley, October 18, 1862.
19. Ibid.

20. Dudley, "Three Critical Periods," 46.
21. Ibid.
22. Ibid., 47.
23. Owsley, *King Cotton Diplomacy*, 355.
24. Howard Jones disagrees with the conventional opinion that Antietam turned the tide against the threat of British intervention. Jones presents evidence that the battle of Antietam convinced both Palmerston and Russell that the war had reached a stalemate and therefore intervention or mediation by England and France was even more necessary. See *Union in Peril*, 168–69.
25. For the role of Lewis in leading the cabinet to oppose Russell, Palmerston, and Gladstone in their proposal for intervention, see Jenkins, *Britain and the War*, vol. 2, 179–82; Jones, *Union in Peril*, 189–90.
26. Jenkins, *Britain and the War*, vol. 2, 181.
27. Stern, *When the Guns Roared*, 155–56.
28. Owsley, *King Cotton Diplomacy*, 173.
29. Ibid., 383–84.
30. DU-4573, Dudley to Seward, January 6, 1863.
31. Dudley, "Three Critical Periods," 44–45.
32. Philip S. Foner, *British Labor and the American Civil War* (New York: Holmes and Meier, 1981), 47.
33. Ibid., 49.
34. Ibid., 50.
35. Ibid., 51.
36. Ibid., 52.
37. See R. J. M. Blackett, "Pressure from Without: African Americans, British Public Opinion and Civil War Diplomacy," in May, *Union, Confederacy, and Atlantic Rim*, 69–97.
38. DU-4573, Dudley dispatch to Seward, March 6, 1862.
39. Stern, *When the Guns Roared*, 164.

CHAPTER 7: THE CONFEDERATE RAMS
1. Bulloch, *Secret Service*, vol. 1, 411–12.
2. DU-4573, Dudley to Seward, August 30, 1862.
3. Ibid., Dudley to Seward, October 16, 1862.
4. Ibid., Dudley to Seward, March 29, 1863.
5. Wallace and Gillespie, *Moran Journal*, vol. 2, January 16, 1863, 1108.
6. DU-4573, Dudley to Seward, February 28, 1863.
7. Ibid., Dudley to Seward, March 29, 1863.
8. Ibid., Adams to Dudley, September 18, 1862.

9. See Maynard, "Forbes-Aspinwall Mission," 67–89.

10. Ibid., 72.

11. Ibid., 73–74.

12. Ibid., 74.

13. Ibid., 75.

14. Jenkins, *Britain and the War,* vol. 2, 249.

15. Ibid., 251.

16. Ibid., 252.

17. Quoted by Sanders, "Lincoln's Consuls," 83, Adams to Seward, April 7, 1863.

18. DU-4573, Seward to Dudley, April 25, 1863.

19. Jenkins, *Britain and the War,* vol. 2, 257.

20. Quoted by Jenkins, *Britain and the War,* vol. 2, 254.

21. DU-4573, Dudley to Lord Russell, January 11, 1864.

22. Ibid., Dudley to Seward, May 2, 1863.

23. For details of the *Alexandra* case, see Crook, *North, South and Powers,* 299–301.

24. Jenkins, *Britain and the War,* vol. 2, 275.

25. Dudley, "Three Critical Periods," 51.

26. Jenkins, *Britain and the War,* vol. 2, 284.

27. Dudley Collection at the Huntington Library contains all the affidavits submitted by Dudley on the rams and other Confederate gunboats under construction in Scotland.

28. DU-4573, Dudley to Seward, July 21, 1863.

29. Quoted by Adams, *Britain and the Civil War,* 144.

30. Dudley, "Three Critical Periods," 52–53.

31. See Jenkins, *Britain and the War,* vol. 2, chap. 11, for an excellent summary of events and diplomatic decision making by Russell and Palmerston leading to the seizure of the Confederate rams.

32. Quoted by Dyer, "Thomas H. Dudley," 407.

CHAPTER 8: FINAL DAYS OF THE *FLORIDA* AND *ALABAMA*

1. McPherson, *Battle Cry of Freedom,* 547–48.

2. Stern, *Confederate Navy,* 128, 140–41.

3. Ibid., 213–16.

4. Semmes, *Memoirs,* 647.

5. Ibid., 708–10; DU-67, affidavit by Henry William Alcott signed on November 24, 1871.

6. Semmes, *Memoirs,* 746.

7. Ibid., 749–50.

8. Stern, *When the Guns Roared,* 281–82.
9. Ibid., 343.
10. *ORN,* ser. 1, vol. 3, 648, Cherbourg, June 14, 1864.
11. Stern, *Confederate Navy,* 89.
12. Quoted by Stern, *When the Guns Roared,* 284.
13. Stern, *Confederate Navy,* 190–91.
14. See Arthur Sinclair, *Two Years on the* Alabama (Boston: 1896), 274.
15. Ibid., 281.
16. For conflicting descriptions of the sea battle between the *Kearsarge* and the *Alabama,* see official reports by Winslow, *ORN,* ser. 1, vol. 3, 59–82; Semmes, *Memoirs,* 647–68. Also John McIntosh Kell, *Recollections of a Naval Life* (Washington, D.C.: The Neal Co., 1900).
17. Quoted by J. M. Browne, *The Story of the* Kearsarge *and the* Alabama (San Francisco: 1868), 13.
18. Stern, *Confederate Navy,* 193.
19. Ibid., 195.
20. DU-4456, Winslow to Dudley, June 24, 1864.
21. DU-2576.
22. Bulloch, *Secret Service,* vol. 1, 287.

CHAPTER 9: THE FAILURE OF CONFEDERATE FOREIGN STRATEGY

1. Parliamentary Debates, Commons, ser. 3, vol. 172, 1254–72.
2. See Owsley, *King Cotton Diplomacy,* 452–56.
3. Jenkins, *Britain and the War,* vol. 2, 313, 316.
4. Ibid., 313.
5. Ibid., 314.
6. DU-2667.
7. DU-2567.
8. DU-2568.
9. Sanders, "Lincoln's Consul," 133–39.
10. Crook, *North, South and Powers,* 301; Jenkins, *Britain and the War,* vol. 2, 323.
11. DU-4573, Dudley to Seward, April 10, 1864.
12. Ibid., Sumner to Dudley, January 24, 1864.
13. Ibid., Bright to Dudley, September 5, 1864.
14. See letter from Bulloch to Mallory, February 17, 1864, *ORN,* ser. 2, vol. 2, 583.
15. Stern, *When the Guns Roared,* 255–56.
16. See "The Shenandoah—Last Confederate Raider," in Stern, *Confederate Navy.*

17. Ibid., 249–53.
18. Ibid.
19. Potts, "Thomas H. Dudley," 19.

CHAPTER 10: CONSUL DUDLEY STAYS ON

1. Quoted by Dyer, "Thomas H. Dudley," 404.
2. Ibid., 407.
3. Dudley, "Three Critical Periods," 42–43.
4. For details of *Alabama* claims diplomacy, see Martin Duberman, *Charles Francis Adams, 1807–1886* (Boston: Houghton-Mifflin, 1960), 323–28, 341–51. A complete record of *Alabama* claims evidence, mostly prepared by Dudley, can be found in "United States before the Tribunal."
5. Sumner speech quoted in Potts, "Thomas H. Dudley," 22.
6. Hofstadter, Miller, and Aaron, *United States,* 618.
7. Duberman, *Charles Francis Adams,* 383.
8. Stern, *When the Guns Roared,* 250.
9. Potts, "Thomas H. Dudley," 25–26.
10. Moran quoted by Dyer, "Thomas H. Dudley," 409.
11. Potts, "Thomas H. Dudley," 27.

BIBLIOGRAPHICAL NOTE

PRIMARY RESEARCH FOR THIS SHORT HISTORY OF THOMAS H. DUDLEY AND the Liverpool network during the American Civil War was carried out at the Huntington Library, San Marino, California, where Dudley's papers are on file. All quotations of Dudley's come from this collection, which includes the official dispatches of the U.S. Consulate at Liverpool from June 1861 to December 1872. Among other items to be found in the Huntington Library collection are dispatches from the Department of State to Thomas Dudley; Confederate correspondence intercepted by the U.S. Secret Service; and personal correspondence between Dudley and prominent British and American public figures during the Civil War period. Additional research was conducted at the Harvard Widener Library, the libraries of the University of California, Berkeley, and the University of Oregon, Eugene, and the public libraries of Boston and San Francisco.

I have made extensive use of the main biographical source on Dudley drawn upon by subsequent historians: William John Potts's "Biographical Sketch of the Late Hon. Thomas H. Dudley," paper read before the American Philosophical Society, Philadelphia, April 19, 1895, reprinted from *Proceedings of the American Philosophical Society* 34 (June 14, 1895). In addition, I have drawn upon the two autobiographical articles written by Dudley himself: "Three Critical Periods in Our Diplomatic Relations with England during the Late War: Personal Recollections of Thomas H. Dudley, Late United States Consul at Liverpool," *Pennsylvania Magazine of History and Biography* 17, no. 1 (1893); and "The Inside Facts of Lincoln's Nomination," *Century Magazine*

(1890), reprinted in *Civil War History* 1, no. 1 (March 1995): 477–79. A brief biographical essay on Thomas Dudley by Brainerd Dyer in *Civil War History* I, no. 4 (December 1955), also proved useful.

I am particularly indebted to Philip Van Doren Stern, who was the first historian to give full credit to the role played by Thomas Dudley in Civil War diplomacy. Dudley is a major actor in Stern's fine book, *When the Guns Roared: World Aspects of the American Civil War* (Garden City, NY: 1965). Also invaluable is Stern's classic *The Confederate Navy: A Pictorial History.* I am equally indebted to Brian Jenkins and his two-volume work, *Britain and the War for the Union* (Montreal: McGill-Queens University Press, 1980). Jenkins's exhaustive research in the British, American, and Canadian diplomatic archives makes him one of the foremost historians of Civil War diplomacy.

The most valuable sources for the two major figures in Confederate naval history are the memoirs of James D. Bulloch and Raphael Semmes: Bulloch's *The Secret Service of the Confederate States in Europe; or, How the Confederate Cruisers Were Equipped,* 2 vols. (London: 1959); and Semmes's *Memoirs of Service Afloat during the War Between the States* (London: 1869).

I found very useful information in the doctoral dissertation by Neil Fred Sanders, "Lincoln's Consuls in the British Isles, 1861–1865" (University of Missouri, 1971). Although Sanders underestimates the danger of war between Britain and the United States during the Civil War period, his work contains excellent research on the establishment of the Northern intelligence network in Britain.

For an understanding of Northern political developments leading up to Lincoln's election, I found Eric Foner's *Free Soil, Free Labor, Free Men: The Ideology of the Republican Party before the Civil War* (New York: Oxford University Press, 1970) to be the best book on the subject. Similarly, James McPherson's *Battle Cry of Freedom: The Civil War Era* (New York: Oxford University Press, 1988) is probably the best and most recent one-volume history of the Civil War available. I also found invaluable the work of Philip S. Foner, *British Labor and the American Civil War* (New York: Holmes and Meier, 1981).

I have drawn upon the scholarship of Norman Ferris, *The Trent Affair: A Diplomatic Crisis* (Knoxville: University of Tennessee Press, 1977); and two monographs by Douglas Maynard: "Union Efforts to Prevent the Escape of the *Alabama,*" *Mississippi Valley Historical Review* 16, no. 1 (June 1954), and "The Forbes-Aspinwall Mission," *Mississippi Valley Historical Review* 45, no. 1 (1958). The account of the ferry boat explosion in which Thomas Dudley came close to losing his life can be found in the *New York Herald,* March 17, 1856.

Other books that proved useful for information on the international aspects of the American Civil War include: Ephraim D. Adams, *Great Britain and the American Civil War*, 2 vols. (New York: Russell and Russell, 1925); D. P. Crook, *The North, the South and the Powers 1861–1865* (New York: Wiley, 1974); and G. D. Lillibridge, *Beacon of Freedom: The Impact of American Democracy upon Great Britain* (Philadelphia: University of Pennsylvania Press, 1955). I also found some very interesting passages in: LaFayette Charles Baker, *The United States Secret Service in the Late War* (Philadelphia: 1890); David Donald, *Charles Sumner and the Rights of Man* (New York: Knopf, 1970); and David Donald, ed., *Why the North Won the Civil War* (New York: Collier, 1960). For a contemporary analysis of international aspects of the Civil War, see Robert E. May, ed., *The Union, the Confederacy, and the Atlantic Rim* (South Bend, Indiana: Purdue University, 1955).

For the diplomacy of the North, see William Henry Seward, *The Diplomatic History of the War for the Union*, vol. 5 (Boston: 1884); and Normal Ferris, *Desperate Diplomacy: William H. Seward's Foreign Policy, 1861* (Knoxville, Tennessee: 1976). For the diplomacy of the South, Frank L. Owsley, see *King Cotton Diplomacy: Foreign Relations of the Confederate States of America* (Chicago: University of Chicago Press, 1931); and James Spence, *The American Union* (London: 1861).

A number of excellent biographies tell the story of some of the key actors described in this book: Charles Francis Adams, Jr., *Charles Francis Adams by His Son* (Boston: 1900); Martin B. Duberman, *Charles Francis Adams, 1807–1886* (Boston: 1960); Henry Adams, *The Education of Henry Adams: An Autobiography* (Boston: Houghton Mifflin Company, 1918); and Worthington C. Ford, ed., *A Cycle of Adams Letters* (Boston: 1920). For England, see H. C. F. Bell, *Lord Palmerston*, 2 vols. (London: 1936); George Trevelyan, *The Life of John Bright* (Boston: 1913); and R. A. J. Walling, ed., *The Diaries of J. Bright* (New York: 1930). For Lord Russell, see Spencer Walpole, *Life of Lord Russell* (London: 1891). Parliamentary speeches of the period can be found in *Hansard's Parliamentary Debates*, 3rd ser. (London: T. C. Hansand, 1830–91).

Reminiscences and memoirs of historical participants in the Civil War period include: Frederick W. Seward, *Reminiscences of a Wartime Statesman and Diplomat, 1830–1915* (New York: Putnam's and Sons, 1916); Sarah A. Wallace and Frank Gillespie, eds., *The Journal of Benjamin Moran* (Chicago: University of Chicago Press, 1949); David Donald, ed., *Inside Lincoln's Cabinet: The Civil War Diaries of Salmon Chase* (New York: 1954); John McIntosh Kell, *Recollections of a Naval Life* (Washington, D.C.: 1900); Arthur Sinclair, *Two Years on the Alabama* (Boston: 1896); and Frank Warren Hackett, *Reminiscences of the Geneva Tribunal of Arbitration, 1872* (Boston: 1911).

Naval history of the Civil War can be found in: Frank J. Merli, *Great Britain and the Confederate Navy, 1861–1865* (Bloomington, Indiana: 1965); and Howard P. Nash, Jr., *A Naval History of the Civil War* (New York: 1972). A wealth of material is contained in the multivolume *Official Records of the Union and Confederate Navies in the War of the Rebellion (ORN)*, 30 vols. (Washington, D.C.: U.S. Government Printing Office, 1894–1922).

INDEX

NOTE: Page references in *italic* type indicate photographs or illustrations. The denotation "*ps*" followed by a number indicates a plate in this series between pp. 70 and 71.